THE OPTIONS WHEEL STRATEGY

THE COMPLETE GUIDE TO BOOST YOUR PORTFOLIO AN EXTRA 15-20% WITH CASH SECURED PUTS AND COVERED CALLS

FREEMAN PUBLICATIONS

© **Copyright 2021 - All rights reserved.**

The content contained within this book may not be reproduced, duplicated or transmitted without direct written permission from the author or the publisher.

Under no circumstances will any blame or legal responsibility be held against the publisher, or author, for any damages, reparation, or monetary loss due to the information contained within this book, either directly or indirectly.

Legal Notice:

This book is copyright protected. It is only for personal use. You cannot amend, distribute, sell, use, quote or paraphrase any part, or the content within this book, without the consent of the author or publisher.

Disclaimer Notice:

The following work is presented for informational purposes only. None of the information herein constitutes an offer to sell or buy any security or investment vehicle, nor does it constitute an investment recommendation of a legal, tax, accounting or investment recommendation by Freeman Publications, its employees or paid contributors. The information is presented without regard for individual investment preferences or risk parameters and is general, non-tailored, non-specific information.

Freeman Publications, including all employees and paid contributors, agree not to trade in any security they write about for a minimum of three days (72 hours) following publication of a new article, book, report or email. Except for existing orders that were in place before submission (any such orders will also always be disclosed inside the document). This includes equity, options, debt, or other instruments directly related to that security, stock, or company. The author may have indirect positions in some companies mentioned due to holdings in mutual funds, ETFs, Closed End Funds or other similar vehicles, and there is no guarantee that the author is aware of the individual portfolios of any of those funds at any given time. Such indirect holdings will generally not be disclosed.

Warning: There is no magic formula to getting rich, in the financial markets or otherwise. Investing often involves high risks and you can lose a lot of money. Success in investment vehicles with the best prospects for price appreciation can only be achieved through proper and rigorous research and analysis. Please do not invest with money you cannot afford to lose. The opinions in this content are just that, opinions of the authors. We are a publishing company and the opinions, comments, stories, reports, advertisements and articles we publish are for informational and educational purposes only; nothing herein should be considered personalized investment advice. Before you make any investment, check with your investment professional (advisor). We urge our readers to review the financial statements and prospectus of any company they are interested in. We are not responsible for any damages or losses arising from the use of any information herein. Past performance is not a guarantee of future results.

This work is based on SEC filings, current events, interviews, corporate press releases, and what we've learned as financial journalists. It may contain errors and you shouldn't make any investment decision based solely on what you read here. It is your money and your responsibility.

Freeman Publications Ltd. are 100% independent in that we are not affiliated with any security, investment vehicle, bank or brokerage house.

All registered trademarks are the property of their respective owners.

CONTENTS

Introduction   11

1. The World's Most Boring, Yet Reliable, Options Strategy   17
2. How The Wheel Works – Step by Step   25
3. Choosing a Broker   40
4. Choosing the Right Candidates   49
5. Technical Analysis for The Wheel (Easier Than You Think)   72
6. How Newer Options Traders Lose Their Shirts - Watch Out for the VIX   93
7. Greeks for The Wheel in 15 Minutes   98
8. Executing the Wheel Strategy: Putting It All Together   106
9. Adjustments for Short-Term Investors   115
10. Money Management   124
11. Increase Your Odds of Success   134

Conclusion   143
Afterword   147
Continuing Your Journey   149
Other Books by Freeman Publications (available on Amazon & Audible)   151
References   153

HOW TO GET THE MOST OUT OF THIS BOOK

To help you along your investing journey, we've created a free bonus companion course that includes spreadsheets, bonus video content, and additional resources that will help you get the best possible results. For this book in particular, we have a number of Bitcoin tutorials in the Bitcoin 101 section.

We highly recommend you sign up now to get the most out of this book. You can do that by going to the link below

https://freemanpublications.com/bonus

Free bonus #1: Company Valuation 101 video course ($97 value)

In this 8-part video course, you'll discover our process for accurately valuing a company. This will help you determine if a stock is overvalued, correctly valued, or a bargain, and give you an indication for when and if to buy it.

Free bonus #2: Guru Portfolios Analyzed ($37 value)

In these videos, we analyze the stock portfolios of Billionaire investors like Warren Buffett as well as top entrepreneurs like Bill Gates.

Free bonus #3: 2 Stocks to Sell Right Now ($17 value)

These 2 stocks are in danger of plummeting in the next 12 months. They are both popular with retail investors, and one is even in the top 5 most held stocks on Robinhood. Believe us; you do not want to be holding these in 2021 and beyond.

Free bonus #4: AI Disruptor - The $4 Stock Poised to be the Next Big Thing in Computing ($17 value)

This under-the-radar company, which less than 1% of investors have heard of, is at the forefront of a breakthrough technology that will change our lives as we know them. Soon, this technology will be in every smartphone, tablet and laptop on the planet.

Free bonus #5: Options 101 ($17 Value)

Options don't have to be risky. In fact, they were invented to *reduce* risk. It's no wonder that smart investors like Warren Buffett regularly use options to supplement their long-term portfolio. In this quick-start guide, we
show you how options work and why they are tools to be utilized rather than feared.

Free bonus #6: The 1 Dividend Stock to Buy and Hold for the Rest of Your Life ($17 Value)

Dividends are the lifeblood of any income investor, and this stock is the cornerstone of any dividend strategy - a true dividend aristocrat with consistent payouts for over 50 years, which you'll surely want to add to your portfolio.

Free bonus #7: Top 3 Growth Stocks for 2021 ($17 Value)

Our 2020 selections outperformed the S&P 500 by 154%. Now we've released our top 3 picks for 2021.

Free bonus #8: Bitcoin 101 ($17 Value)

How to safely buy and store Bitcoin, even if you're a complete beginner. Contains video walkthroughs of everything you need for a stress free Bitcoin experience.

All of these bonuses are 100% free, with no strings attached. You don't need to provide any personal details except your email address.

To get your bonuses, go to:
https://freemanpublications.com/bonus

To David, because this is the only way I know how to appropriately thank you.

INTRODUCTION

The stock market has always attracted people who are looking to get rich. Speculative forces in the market have dictated short-term price moves for over a century now, and it's unfortunate that all stock market activity is often painted as one large speculative play. New entrants to the market think all they need to do to make money is buy when a stock will go up and then exit before it goes down. However, reality soon sets in once they put their money on the line.

Our answer to the "How do I make money in stocks?" question has always been the same. The best method is a long-term buy and hold strategy in which you behave like an investor in a business. Dividends can supercharge your returns in that time period while alternative assets like gold and cryptocurrencies will hedge your portfolio against inflation and any untoward occurrences with the US dollar.

So where do options fall into this? Options are often highlighted as examples of speculative financial instruments. Most intelligent investors, we're told, stay away from them for fear they can go wrong in a hurry. This is true. However, we'd like to point out that options go wrong when you don't understand how they work, or their intended strategies. You can make options as complex as possible or you can use them in simple, reliable ways.

One of the qualities that makes options trading so enticing is the ability to generate income. For the longest time, bonds and dividend stocks were viewed as the only safe sources of income, but this isn't true. Options, when used in a sound strategy, have the ability to make you just as much money, if not more, than dividends. And the strategy we present in this book can enable you to earn that money with a much smaller base of capital.

Executing such strategies requires a lot of patience and a willingness to slowly compound your money. This approach is opposed to the often advertised "collect 200%+ returns every year" day trading methods that will have you running huge risks with your capital. In our view, minimizing risk is far more important than shooting for huge gains.

In the professional money management world, risk-adjusted gains matter more than absolute returns. After all, anyone can generate 100% returns if they're risking 150% per trade! Generating 15-20% returns while risking just one percent or less of your capital is far tougher. Adopting a lower risk approach ensures you won't lose money when you do lose, which is the first step to making long term gains.

The strategy we're going to explain in this book, called The Wheel, is a simple one that uses options conservatively. You're going to learn how to construct a portfolio that will generate anywhere between 15-25% per year in additional income. If your aim is to generate 100% or some astronomical figure on your capital, we're sorry to say that we can't help you with that.

Our strategy is low risk, and some would even say boring. Don't mistake this to mean it's ineffective. When it comes to the stock market, boring beats exciting. In fact, if you've traded options before, you'll recognize many of the terms and components of The Wheel.

However, the true power of our strategy lies in its ability to generate income consistently, without having you absorb additional risk. There are very few strategies that can make similar claims. Consistency and scalability are important for every investment strategy and the Wheel checks both boxes. Although it works whether you have just $1,000 in your account or $1 million.

We recommend that you have a basic portfolio in place before implementing The Wheel. We're doing this to reduce your risk even further and ensure you'll always have some portion of your money bringing you returns no matter what. While The Wheel is a great strategy to make money, it's best to use it within a larger risk-minimized framework.

The Wheel uses options and it's understandable if you have objections to trading them. Many long-term investors have been scared away from options by the uninformed financial media. You've been led to think they're doomsday devices. However, the truth is far more subtle.

Options are merely tools. Just as a knife can be used to cause harm or used for good, options can be used in the wrong ways to cause staggering losses.

There have been many instances of famous investors using options to boost their gains or even construct entire portfolios from them. Let's start with the biggest of them all, Warren Buffett. He has been quoted as calling derivatives "financial WMDs" in the past, so you'd think he'd stay well away from options. However, he routinely buys and sells puts to generate income for Berkshire Hathaway. It isn't a strategy he uses very often, but if he's carrying large amounts of cash, he puts it to work by selling puts and collecting premiums.

Buffett is an example of someone who conservatively uses options. On the other end of the spectrum, the 2008 financial crisis saw Jamie Mai and Charlie Ledley of Cornwall Capital turn $110,000 into $136 million before they went on to call the top of the American housing market. Their feats were detailed in Michael Lewis's book *The Big Short*. Mai and Ledley used options to build their capital by placing bets on asymmetric opportunities, where the reward was far greater than the risk. Options trades can be designed to reward such situations, and they made the most of it.

Edward O. Thorp is a well-known name to anyone who has played blackjack. The author of *Beat the Dealer* was also a prolific options trader who averaged 20% per year over a 30-year period trading options.

And perhaps the best example of an options trade was made outside the financial markets by George Lucas (Artemis Capital Management

LP, 2016). The creator of *Star Wars* famously chose to forego his $750,000 director's fee in exchange for the rights to merchandising, sequels, and licensing the *Star Wars* franchise. The rest is history, and Lucas cashed his rights in when Disney bought the franchise for $4 billion in 2015. Deciding to buy the rights instead of cash is an options trade, in essence.

We're not claiming you can turn nothing into $4 billion by reading this book. In fact, we're cautioning against thinking like this. However, we can assure you that the strategy in this book has the potential to make you an additional 15-25% per year without additional risk to your portfolio. It will augment whatever income you already collect on your stock holdings.

You don't need massive capital or special expertise. It's best if you're familiar with the stock market and further understand how options work. After all, it's tough to implement an options trading strategy if you don't understand what a call or a put is. We'll have you shorting options in this book, so you will need to understand the implications of that.

You'll also need to know your broker requirements for options trading approval. This book will help you with that.

We'll explain all possible implications as much as possible. However, if you are brand new to options, then we recommend checking out our free guide *Options 101*, which you can download by going to

https://freemanpublications.com/bonus

If you are familiar with, or have experience trading the covered call and cash-secured put strategies, you will be a step ahead; but don't worry, we'll be describing them in detail.

Lastly, we ask that you exercise a lot of patience when learning this strategy. It might be simple, but don't confuse this for being easy. Although the technical aspects of this strategy aren't tough, executing it with patience and discipline is. It takes time for The Wheel to truly produce fruits and you need to be willing to give it time to grow.

You'll find that you can use The Wheel strategy on just about any investment vehicle that is optionable. Throughout this book, we'll often refer to "stocks", but know that we mean the broader array of financial instruments that includes ETFs and other Exchange Traded Products. We'll also talk of "trades" or trading. By no means are we implying day trading or any time frame with those terms. We are simply referring to a transaction conducted on a securities exchange.

So having said all that, let's move forward and take a look at what The Wheel is and how it works.

1

THE WORLD'S MOST BORING, YET RELIABLE, OPTIONS STRATEGY

So what is The Wheel Strategy, and why is it so powerful? To begin with, you're not going to experience the stereotypical rollercoaster of emotions that many investors associate with options. In fact, the Wheel is a straightforward strategy that anyone can execute with just an additional two or three hours per week to dedicate to a portfolio.

With the wheel, you can expect safe and continuous gains no matter the volatility or unpredictability in the stock market. What's more, the gains you can earn will outpace traditional dividend investing. Currently the average dividend yield on an S&P 500 stock is just 1.48%, with the average yield for a Dividend Aristocrat stock just 3.5%. The Wheel can generate annual returns far greater than that, without additional risk.

The Wheel is also referred to as the Triple Income Strategy or "Buy and Hold on Steroids." This is because there are three income components in the strategy.

- Income #1 - You collect the premium from selling cash-secured puts
- Income #2 - You collect the premium from selling covered calls
- Income #3 - You collect cash when your covered call gets assigned and you sell your shares

As you can see, The Wheel requires you to sell cash-covered puts (CSPs) and write covered calls (CCs). Let's examine these in more detail.

EXPLORING THE WHEEL

To understand The Wheel, you need to fully understand what cash-secured puts and covered calls are.

The cash-secured put (CSP) is a great way to get paid to enter a trade. Here's how it works. Let's say you wish to own a stock but would like to generate additional cash upon entry. You sell (write) a put that is exercisable at a print that is close to the price at which you would like to pay to buy the stock. Because you are selling an option, you collect a payment, called the premium. Because the put is close to the money (meaning close to the current market price of the stock), the premium will be significant. If the put finishes in the money (ITM), you'll be required to buy the stock.

This is fine because you originally wanted to own the stock. However, if the put finishes at a price that makes it worthless, referred to as out of the money (OTM), you can repeat the process - write another CSP and collect a premium once again. Eventually you will be buying the stock, and then be able to wait for your investment to mature. However, cash-secured puts are a great way to boost your investment returns in advance of that purchase.

Once you own the stock, you can begin to sell covered calls (CC). A CC is a two-part trade where you own the underlying stock and write a call against it, typically at an OTM strike price. Because you're writing an option, you'll collect the premium on it. If the option moves ITM at expiration, you will be "assigned" and have to sell your stock. (No problem – just sell another put option on the same stock and repeat the process!) However, if you write the call at a price that is well outside the money upon the option's expiration, you get to keep your stock as well as the premium.

The CC can be used as a speculative strategy as well. You can buy a stock and write a call that is close to the money. If the price of the stock rises to ensure the option finishes ITM, you get to keep the premium and sell the underlying stock for a profit. It's hard to make this speculative strategy work over the long term because you can't predict market moves, but the covered call can be a great way to earn additional gains on existing portfolio holdings.

In essence, CSPs pay you to buy shares you like, while CCs can pay you to sell shares that you wish to sell. Trading like this isn't sexy or exciting. Over the course of a year, this approach can translate into a significant addition to your cash reserves. Over five years or a decade, the returns will add up significantly, especially when you take compounding into account.

Earning a 20% return depends on stock selection, your experience, and most of all, your willingness to stay the course and patiently execute your strategies. It's pretty boring but it passes the ultimate test, in our eyes. You'll be able to sleep well at night.

Who Is This for?

The Wheel is for anybody who wants to boost returns and earn additional cash on an existing portfolio. Retirees or those who are income-oriented in their portfolio will benefit massively from this strategy. You can collect additional income on top of your dividends. While the returns might vary, depending on the makeup of your portfolio, you can rest assured that it is a consistent stream of income when you follow the steps and advice we describe in this book.

We've always said that options should be used as an additional to your core portfolio, not as a substitution. The Wheel is no different and is best used by people who have a base portfolio in place.

Here's a sample portfolio allocation for retirement:

- 40% of your portfolio in *Dividend Growth Investing* stocks/ETFs/Closed End Funds (CEFs)
- 25% in bonds
- 15% dedicated to The Wheel
- 10% in higher growth stocks with no dividend payment
- 5% gold
- 5% crypto

If you are young and just beginning to build a portfolio, you might allocate funds with these percentages:

- 25% in *Dividend Growth Investing* stocks/funds/Closed End Funds
- 15% dedicated to The Wheel
- 50% in higher growth stocks with no dividend payment
- 5% gold
- 5% crypto

These percentages will vary depending on your investment goals, but we recommend assigning a small portion of your portfolio to The Wheel. We've noted 15% for those with an existing portfolio, but it can be as high as 25% if income is your primary goal.

A huge benefit of The Wheel, particularly for those just beginning to build a portfolio, is that it can lower your cost basis of stock ownership – rather than buying shares outright, you sell puts and acquire the shares through assignment. Over the long term, you could effectively end up owning your favorite stock for free, by continuing to sell puts and calls.

Note that this strategy isn't a magic bullet. It isn't something you can generate astronomical returns with, especially if you don't have lots of capital. For example, to execute The Wheel on Amazon stock, your broker would require you to have $340,000 in your account just to sell cash-secured puts.

We would also like to point out that every investment strategy does have risks attached to it. The Wheel has previously been termed a covered call on steroids. This description makes it seem as if you can attain all the benefits of the covered call without adding additional risk. While The Wheel does not require you to absorb high levels of risk, it is incorrect to say that there is zero risk.

The Wheel isn't going to give you free money, as beginners often say when they talk about covered calls. There is no such thing as free money. The CSP and CC don't add any risk to your position, and this is why it can seem as if you're earning "free" money. However, the risk of your stock dropping to zero is still a substantial risk that you undertake whenever you commit money in the financial markets.

Why Do Some Sources Claim You Can Earn 100% Annual Returns?

Read about The Wheel Strategy online and you'll come across promises of earning 100% or more returns on your money each and every year. These claims seem very credible because many provide a spreadsheet for you to plug in numbers and project returns. However, once you try to execute the strategy, you'll realize that earning these kinds of returns is a hit-or-miss prospect.

These spreadsheets assume you'll write options on stocks that have high implied volatility (IV) levels, and therefore high premiums.. While high-IV stocks have a great chance of behaving the way you want them to, they're just as likely to behave in the opposite manner. The high IV tells you that the stock's price is likely to have wide swings. This means you're never going to be sure how your trades are going to end up.

Over the course of a year, you'll find that many of these kinds of trades will go against you, and as a result, achieving 100% returns is pretty much impossible. Of course, this is before we even explore the mental stress such a high risk-to-reward strategy will cause. Instead of aiming for such high returns, it's far better to set your sights lower and collect a decent, more consistent, return on your money.

You will read posts on online forums about how some people claim to be earning 20% per month using The Wheel. Look closer, though, and you'll notice that all of them have been running the strategy for a few months at best, and often in extremely bullish market conditions. In the long run, it's impossible to generate such astronomical returns without risking an unacceptable amount of capital. Do not let these profit claims pull you astray. Stick to the plan we set out for you, and you will do better in the long run.

We're not saying 100% per year is unattainable as a one-off in certain market circumstances. It's just that it's highly unlikely for anyone to consistently achieve these kinds of returns over a decade or longer.

A more realistic number for you to target is 0.3-0.5% per week. This will give you an annualized return between 15-26%. These returns, when compounded over a number of years, are significantly higher than what the average market participant earns.

A market-tracking ETF earns around 9% per year. Even if you earn 15% per year, you're getting more than 150% of what the market gives you routinely. The other thing to remember is that The Wheel works whether the market is bullish, bearish, or neutral. The cash flow you earn during bear markets will boost your overall return immeasurably and will offset the unrealized capital losses in your portfolio.

To drill our point home, we'd like to use a baseball analogy. Let other market participants aim for home runs all the time. It's far better for you to concentrate on hitting singles and doubles consistently.

Freeman Wheel Strategy Rule #1

If it looks too good to be true. It is.

Now that we have set expectations in place, let's move forward and look at how The Wheel works.

2

HOW THE WHEEL WORKS – STEP BY STEP

Experienced options traders will appreciate the simplicity of The Wheel. So why don't more options traders use this approach? The simple answer is that it is a rather unsexy strategy. Professional options traders, who have the entire day to devote to the market, don't find it attractive to spend just two to three hours per week on The Wheel.

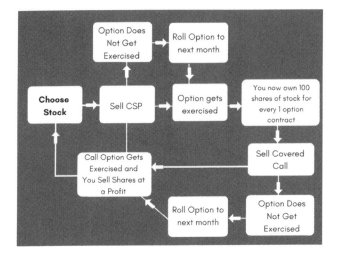

Figure 1: A visual overview of the different stages of The Wheel Strategy

The Wheel is best suited for those who don't have time to monitor the markets closely and want a conservative way of earning a decent return. The way The Wheel enables this is through a multi-step process. As you can see from the diagram, the process can circle around and around, like a wheel, allowing you to earn options premiums again and again

Let's break down each step and see how it works.

STEP ONE: CHOOSE A STOCK

The first step is choosing a stock. This should be one you have researched and are comfortable with its long-term growth prospects. See our books, *The 8 Step Beginner's Guide To Value Investing* and *Dividend Growth Investing* for guidance on selecting quality stocks.

To filter for stocks which work best for the wheel strategy, we cover this in depth inside chapter 4 of this book.

To implement The Wheel strategy you will need a company with listed options. That may sound obvious, but not every stock has an active options market. Recent IPOs, for example, are not viable choices.

STEP TWO: SELLING CASH-SECURED PUTS

When you sell (write) a put, you are taking on the obligation to buy at a particular price, called the strike. Every time a put is sold, someone is on the other side of the transaction, taking a "long" put position. Long puts give a person the right to sell stock at the strike price, maybe even before the expiration date. By writing a put, then, you are entering into a contract where you must buy the stock for the strike price if it expires ITM, or if the holder of the long position decides "to put it to you". The holder of the long side pays the premium that you get to keep, no matter what price the stock may reach when the put either expires or is assigned to you.

Let's look at an example with AT&T. At the time of this writing, the stock was trading at $28.77. Let's assume you have no qualms about owning it at this price. You think its long-term prospects are great and therefore you write a put with a strike price of $28.50, which is the closest ITM strike on AT&T's option chain.

Remember, writing a put means you will have to buy the stock at the strike -- $28.50 -- if the long put holder exercises the option. Let's assume the current price for your put is $0.60 per contract and it will expire in 30 days. (One contract will obligate you to buy 100 shares if the put is exercised.) Therefore $60 will be deposited into your account straight away ($0.60 * 100)

Here's where the "cash" portion of the strategy enters. Because you're writing puts, your broker is going to limit your risk exposure and require you to have cash in hand to buy AT&T in case it finishes ITM – at or below the $28.50. This means you'll need to have enough cash to buy 100 shares of AT&T (if you wrote one put; if you wrote two puts, you'll need cash for 200 shares).

Your put's strike price is $28.50, so you'll need $2,850 as cash in your account to execute one CSP on AT&T. This may seem like a pretty large amount to have just sitting in cash, but it is enabling you to carry out this strategy. This is why we mentioned earlier that it's best to use The Wheel as a secondary income generation strategy and not a primary one.

If you like AT&T's long term prospects, but don't have the money to buy 100 shares, , then you must decide if you want to simply buy some shares now, or wait until you have the cash.

However, waiting has an opportunity cost. Let's say it takes you a year to gather $2,850, but during that time, AT&T's stock price has rocketed 50% higher. Now you'll need $4,275 to write a CSP! If you've done proper research into a stock, and believe it to be a good investment, you will probably do better buying as many shares as you can afford, rather than waiting.

Using the number in our example, if you have the $2,850 in your account, you'll earn $60 for the CSP in a month (remember we said we assume the put expires in 30 days). That's 2.1% or around 25% annualized. Compare this to the 50% potential capital gain you've left on the table and you'll see that waiting is a poor choice, from an opportunity cost perspective. Later in this book we'll be going into the minimum acceptable strike price for both your CSP and CC to make executing The Wheel worth your time.

If you don't have the money to write a CSP on a given stock, buy the stock as best as you can and then search for other CSP candidates. The cash return you'll earn from a CSP will always pale compared to the capital gains you'll receive from a long-term investment holding.

If you don't have the money to write a CSP on a given stock, then you must decide how committed you are to the long-term prospects of the company. Do you buy a few shares now, or do you wait? Other opportunities can always be found, and you can search for them while you are building your cash reserves. You must remember though, that the cash percentage return you'll earn with The Wheel strategy pale compared to the capital gains you'll receive from a long-term investment holding.

Expiration and Assignment

Let's assume you do have the cash that your broker requires, and you have written a CSP. All options expire at some point in time, and there are two possible results. The first is that the option finishes OTM and the second is that the option finishes ITM. (An ATM finish is treated the same as an ITM one.)

Let's examine what happens in the first case.

If the CSP option finishes OTM, meaning the stock's market price is greater than the put's strike price, you get to keep the premium and your cash balance remains intact. You won't have the option assigned to you. This leaves you free to write another CSP and ride it to expiration (also called expiry). With this strategy as with most written options, it's frequently best to pick an expiration that is between 21-45 days away. We'll discuss the reasons in detail later in this book. For now, understand that when you write an option, you are selling time, and the more time until the expiration date, the more you should be paid.

This plan means every CSP you write will last for around a month. Some traders write options that expire in only a week for high-IV stocks. High-IV stocks have larger premiums attached to their options and this makes up for the lack of time decay on a weekly option. Unless you want to spend a lot of time monitoring the trade, we recommend that you stick to the 21-45 days.

Now that you have a CSP, you have the risk is that the option finishes ITM (or ATM). So what happens in this scenario?

Your broker will assign you the option, which means you'll have to buy the stock at the strike price. Because you have the cash necessary to cover this purchase, buying the stock isn't an issue. A CSP is therefore a win-win for everyone involved. You get to own the stock that you're keen on, essentially at a lower price than what you would have paid had you bought the stock outright. If the stock price rises to a small extent and the option finishes OTM, you've earned a small premium on your investment and can write another CSP.

The only risk with the CSP is that the underlying stock rises by a huge extent. This means you'll have missed the capital gains in exchange for a small premium. This scenario often happens with highly volatile stocks. We'll later explain how you can screen out such risky stocks when implementing this strategy.

For now, you can see how the CSP is a great way to be bullish on a stock and get paid to enter a position. Note that the CSP is different from a cash covered put. A cash covered put is initialized when you already own the stock in question and write puts against it. A CSP "covers" you via the cash you hold in your account.

STEP THREE: AFTER THE CSP EXPIRES

Depending on where your CSP finishes, you'll either initiate a new CSP or buy the underlying stock. This step isn't very complicated and can be done with just the click of a button (brokers will automatically transact the stock purchase when you are assigned). Some traders move on from the original stock and initiate a new position in another stock. To us, this doesn't make much sense.

Remember that you should initiate CSPs only on stocks that you're keen on owning. Do not make the mistake of writing CSPs on random stocks because you think they won't finish ITM. This is a highly speculative strategy that is not an intelligent way of investing. Follow the investment principles we outlined in our previous books and identify the stocks you would love to own. Execute CSPs on those stocks only.

Assuming your option finished ITM, you'll then move on to the next step of the strategy.

STEP FOUR: SELL A COVERED CALL

You now own the stock from the CSP finishing ITM, and are ready to write a covered call. The CC is a two-part trade. The primary, money-making leg is a long stock position, and the second leg is a short call. CCs can be used for both long-term investment as well as short-term income. For an in-depth discussion see our previous book, Covered Calls for Beginners.

Whether you plan to hold the stock long term or short term doesn't matter. All that matters is that you believe the stock has a good future and will trend upwards. Of course, that doesn't mean it needs to skyrocket immediately. In fact those kinds of stocks are not ideal covered call candidates . Instead we are looking for stocks with an overall mildly bullish trend to them.

Later you will read that we recommend "boring" companies for The Wheel. You don't want a stock that tends to move sharply on earnings – the unpredictability makes strike price selection very difficult. However, if yours is not boring and tends to move on earnings, it might be best to wait until after the announcement to write your call.

Also, many stocks see increased interest as the ex-dividend date approaches. Institutions, for example, use complex formulae to target dividend "grabs", where they buy a stock shortly before the ex-dividend date, become eligible to collect the dividend, and then sell the stock immediately afterwards. Before you write that call, then, make sure you've evaluated the stock's dividend schedule and price action patterns around important dates. Technical analysis of the stock can help, and we'll offer some guidance in Chapter 5.

Once you've decided on a strike price, you will also need to choose an expiration date. Remember, the more time you have the option open, the more you should get paid, but we recommend that you stay within that 21-45 day window. If the call is assigned to you, you have stock ownership to "cover" it, hence the name.

Here are two scenarios that can play out in this trade.

Scenario One

The first scenario is the most negative one. Let's say your analysis was incorrect and the stock declines instead of rising. In this situation, your call remains OTM, and expires, with you keeping the premium collected, while your stock moves into a loss. However, this loss is offset by the premium you'll earn by writing the call. Here's what the math looks like:

Loss on the trade = Loss from long stock leg - Premium collected from short call

The closer your call was to the money when you wrote it, the greater the premium you stood to earn. If the stock's price decline is small, you may actually have a breakeven situation. You will still own the stock and therefore have the potential to sell another CC.

What happens if the stock loss is NOT small and it keeps declining?

You will need to decide what your conviction is -- if you are convinced that the downturn is temporary, you can continue to hold the stock and sell OTM CCs to collect the premiums. Of course, you'll need to select strike prices that don't risk ITM expirations if you want to keep the stock long term.

If you have lost interest in the stock and want to exit the stock position, you could choose to write the next CC ITM and have the stock called away from you.

If, however, your objective was simply to earn a short-term profit, this is a poor situation indeed. Some traders set stop loss orders at the breakeven point. By setting the order in advance, the broker should automatically sell the stock. Be careful, however, that such a situation doesn't leave you with a "naked" short call, where you no longer own the stock, but you still have the call obligation that you established when you sold the CC. You'll need to check with your broker to determine if the stop loss order will include the sale of the call along with the stock. Remember that each single option contract represents 100 shares. You will not be able to sell CCs if you own less than 100.

This means the covered call is best executed either on stocks you would love to own for the long term and don't mind shelling out cash for, or on low-priced stocks that you believe are under-valued and have good appreciation potential in the short term.

Scenario Two

The second scenario occurs when the stock rises but not so much as to move the call ITM. In this case, your CC will expire worthless and you can then write another CC. Ideally, your stock will rise slowly, steadily over time, and you'll write OTM CCs over and over, generating that extra income. If you decide you no longer want to hold the stock, you'll want to sell by writing a CC with a strike price that will cause the call to be assigned. Thus, you'll earn a profit equal to the strike price (your stock exit price) minus the buying price plus the premium earned by writing the call.

Profit = (Sale price of long stock - Buy price of long stock) + Premium earned by writing call

Choosing strike prices is not as easy as it sounds. How close should the strike be to your stock's current price? When you place your strike price far from your entry, you'll decrease your profits by doing so. On the flip side, you'll earn a higher premium by writing a call that's closer to the money, but risk having the stock called away. The best way to figure out where you ought to place your strike is to explore the options calculator on your broker's software. We'll explain how you can choose the best broker in the next chapter.

For now, understand that it's best to model various scenarios on the calculator to figure out the trade-offs. For example, if the premium you can earn by writing a call closer to the money makes up for the potential gains you'll give up on the long stock, it's worth placing this trade. By minimizing the middle-of-the-road zone, you'll increase your chances of earning your maximum profit. Also remember: if your stock is called away, you can always buy it back!

Managing a Covered Call

There are a few ancillary fees to consider when it comes to the CC. Option assignment is an important factor when designing your strategy. Thanks to the way brokers operate, many traders actively shun assignment and this defines your maximum profit.

Brokers that charge assignment fees can eat into your profits massively. We don't mean to say that such brokers are bad or somehow inefficient. That would be too simplistic. You'll need to focus on the overall package that they offer. However, if you'll be paying assignment fees, check to see how much they'll reduce your profit. You might be better off writing calls that are well OTM, thereby avoiding assignment and fees. Of course, this means that the premium you collect will be smaller, but you will still enjoy the profits of stock's upward move.

Covered calls are an easy trade to manage, but that doesn't mean you can ignore them or your investments. It's your money and you should always pay attention to your portfolio. You'll need to pay particular attention as the expiration date approaches, because you'll be faced with decisions.

What if the call is ITM and you don't want to be assigned? You can always buy back the call. Or, you can "roll" the call by simultaneously buying it back and selling another at a different strike price or expiration date. Even if the call is OTM, you may want to roll it before expiration.

What if your stock has declined, and the call is now significantly OTM? In this scenario, you should buy back your call rather than wait for it to expire, and then write another call a few strikes below.

As with the CSP, you want to write options that are in that 21-45 day window discussed earlier. With every passing day, an option loses value, a concept called time decay, and that decay accelerates as the expiration date gets nearer. You should take full advantage of it.

Your decision to roll your strike prices should be governed by your trade objectives and whether you can evaluate your reasons for entry. If you find that your stock analysis was incorrect, it's best to shut the trade down and evaluate the possibilities with an other stock.

If you want to own the stock for the long haul, then you need to be careful to place your strikes at a good distance away from the current market price so that the stock isn't called away. You don't want to lose long-term price appreciation in exchange for an option premium. The premium will amount to just a few percentage points while the unrealized gains on the stock can be much higher.

MAKING THE WHEEL TURN

Now that you've learned about the CSP and the CC, how can you bring everything together to form The Wheel? For starters, both strategies produce income to a certain extent. However, when you combine the two together, you supercharge the money you can earn from your investment.

The trade begins with you selecting a stock, writing a CSP, and then monitoring how it works out. If the put moves ITM, you keep the premium and buy the stock. This opens the next step of the trade which is the CC. Now that you own the stock, you can sell CCs again and again, keeping the premiums you earn from writing the calls.

When viewed overall, you have two income-producing legs and one long stock leg that should bring you long-term unrealized capital gains. The income legs can add an additional 5 to 10% returns annually and this is what ensures you'll earn an average of 15-20% annually on your portfolio.

The key is to operate in stocks that you want to hold for the long term. While speculative strategies can work, it's best to stick to long-term investments because short-term trades require more monitoring and can be tough to replicate over the long term. We recommend running this strategy with options that have expiry dates a month out, but you can use weekly options as well.

Managing The Wheel is also straightforward when you've adopted a long-term investment approach. If you've properly researched the company, you don't have to worry about your approach to the long stock. You simply keep holding it unless your primary investment thesis turns out to be false. As for the strike prices of the CSP and CC, you can either roll them up or down depending on the way the market behaves.

If your CSP doesn't get assigned, you've profited from the transaction, and you can write another put that might be closer to the money. If the stock you're interested in is on a massive bull run, it's better to simply buy the stock outright instead of trying to acquire it with your CSP. However, such runs happen rarely and you can rest assured that for the most part, a CSP that's written close to the money will usually finish ITM.

Should you write puts that are far OTM? In our opinion, this doesn't make a lot of sense. Your objective with The Wheel should be to ultimately gain ownership of the stock. Writing a CSP that is far OTM doesn't achieve this. Long-term investors will benefit from pushing their calls OTM but not their puts.

To reiterate, here are the three streams of income you can earn with The Wheel:

- Income #1 - you collect the premium from selling puts.
- Income #2 - you collect the premium from selling covered calls.
- Income #3 - you collect the cash when your covered call gets assigned and you sell your shares.

The great thing about The Wheel is that you keep your premiums no matter what. It doesn't matter what happens to the long stock, you keep the premiums you receive from writing options. If the world were to come to an end and everyone sold everything, you'd still keep your premiums. Admittedly, you'd have bigger problems to worry about in that scenario, but it goes to show how certain option premiums are.

Aside from this, there's the obvious benefit that you can earn two streams of income on your investment instead of just one. Usually, investors implement covered calls to generate income, but if you have the cash to buy a stock and then sell a covered call, it makes sense to first put it to use with a CSP. You'll double the income you earn from your trade.

3

CHOOSING A BROKER

As easy as it is to just run The Wheel using your regular broker, it's worth figuring out if there is a better option.

There are a few elements you need to consider before choosing an options broker. Let's look at them one by one.

Trading Commissions and Fees

Commissions and fees are a considerable headwind to overcome when it comes to trading. With options, there are government fees that are the same across all brokers, and then there are two tiers of commissions/fees that will vary from broker to broker. The first tier is the cost of buying and selling options. This cost is similar to the commissions you'll pay when buying or selling stocks. Most brokers will list per contract commissions, but some will have a model where you'll pay a fixed charge up to a certain level of trading activity, and then will pay on a different schedule when you trade above this threshold.

Thanks to the rise in discount brokers, there are many brokers who don't charge commissions to trade options contracts, but will charge fixed contract fees, which means you still end up paying to trade, but it might be just $0.50-$1 per options contract. That sounds like it could get expensive, but most brokers have a maximum price per trade. For example, the contract fees on Tastyworks are capped at $10 regardless of the trade size.

Not every broker will charge you contract fees, so this makes your choice a little more confusing. Take the time to consider your trading volume and look at the commissions and fees schedule that the broker advertises. At the very least, you should expect to pay no trading commissions because there are so many app-based firms that don't charge these.

In the second tier you might pay fees when a call or put is exercised or assigned. Once again, some brokers don't charge for this activity, so you need to consider this cost in your decision analysis. (Options buyers pay exercise fees. Assignment fees are what options sellers pay. It's the same fee, except the name changes depending on which side of the trade you've assumed.)

Add these commissions and fees together to take your final cost to trade into account. One broker might charge zero commissions but higher assignment fees. Remember that these fees eat away at your profits, so you need to be aware of them before trading.

As a rule of thumb, when you're just starting with 1-2 contracts per trade, if your total trade fees (opening/closing/exercise/assignment) add up to more than $15 per trade, you need to find another broker!

SOFTWARE

Broker trading platforms vary greatly. The best brokers to pick are the ones who cater exclusively to active traders. These companies have the most sophisticated tools. Having said that, the platforms that these brokers provide can be quite complex, so you don't want to choose one that requires you to go through a steep learning curve.

Avoid choosing brokers who cater to long-term investors. A tell-tale sign is a lack of services and platform features. Long-term investment is a different game entirely, and most investors don't need sophisticated charting tools or options visualization tools. In fact, many long-term investors don't even need or want a real-time chart.

This is not the case for options traders. You need tools to help you enter proposed strike prices, and you'll clearly be able to see your break even points and maximum profit and loss scenarios.

You don't need standalone desktop terminals to execute these strategies. You'll be spending perhaps a few hours every month maintaining these setups, so it's not as if you need a supercomputer to make them work. A web-based software is more than enough for your needs.

If your broker's charting interface is clunky, you need to find another broker. The competition is keen for your business and serious brokers have elegant software for charting and options trading. If you are not ready to change brokers, then you can use a resource such as tradingview.com or stockcharts.com. These free software sites allow you to draw support and resistance zones, and use technical indicators you'll need when analyzing possible setups. We'll be talking more about technical analysis later in the book.

One more important consideration for you to consider is your broker's experience in dealing with options trading. You should be planning to expand your options trading knowledge and abilities, with The Wheel being just the start. One type of options trade that can be very profitable is the credit spread, where you enter 2 option legs at once. You already know what a spread is – you are effectively creating a spread trade when you roll that CC we discussed earlier. The more experienced brokers will allow you to enter both legs of your spread trades at once. This makes execution and capturing optimal prices much easier than entering each leg one at a time. It also insulates you from sudden bursts of market volatility.

CUSTOMER SERVICE QUALITY

This should go without saying, but you need to choose a broker with a high level of customer service. Unfortunately, these days, most customer service queries are handled by chatbots or an underpaid intern on Twitter. This is frustrating because you'll need to speak to a human every once in a while. Evaluating how quickly you can access a human being is an excellent metric to measure different brokers.

You can check this by typing a few questions into the chatbot software and then checking to see how soon the bot connects you through to a human. If it keeps you going round in circles, then it's a good indication that the company doesn't take customer support seriously enough. Many companies will ask you to leave your number and request a callback. This isn't good enough. If your situation is an emergency, you can hardly be expected to sit around waiting for a phone call from your broker.

Another way of evaluating their service is to send them an email and look at how long they take to get back to you. In most cases, the initial response will be quick. Send a follow-up question and wait for a response. By doing this, you're checking to see what kind of customer service process the company has. Most brokers figure that once initial questions are answered via email, the person asking them ends up opening an account. This leads them to not follow up on secondary emails.

The lack of response indicates poor after-sales service, and you should stay away from such brokers. The longer a broker has been in business, the better their customer service will be.

Choose a broker that has been around for a long time and read their reviews on impartial websites like Trustpilot. Always choose a broker that is registered with the Financial Regulatory Authority or FINRA. If you're just starting out, avoid offshore brokers since all kinds of illegal and unethical behavior is possible with them.

OPTIONS ACCOUNT LEVEL REQUIREMENTS

To trade The Wheel in the U.S., you'll need to obtain approval from your broker, by completing a questionnaire about your investment experience, income, net worth and your trading plans.

Brokers typically have four or five option trading levels, with each successive one allowing more and more types of trades. Writing covered calls can typically be done with a Level 1 account. For cash secured puts though, many brokers require Level 2 account status. As you gain more knowledge about trading options, you will need to obtain a Level 3 or 4 approval to trade more sophisticated strategies.

Trading The Wheel in other countries becomes more complicated if your focus is on U.S. markets and stocks. You'll need to make sure your broker deals in international shares and you'll need to file Form W-8BEN with the U.S. Internal Revenue Service. You'll also have to evaluate the additional fees that may be charged for international shares. The concept of option trading levels is also something to consider. You will need to ask your broker if CSPs are allowed with Level 1 or will you need Level 2 approval.

FEE SCHEDULE

In older times, many brokers could to get away with hiding fees within their fee schedules. This doesn't happen anymore, thanks to the increased transparency that strong competition has created. However, a few hidden fees still sneak in. For example, some brokers may charge an account maintenance fee every month if your total margin is less than $10,000. This isn't advertised as a minimum margin penalty, of course, so most people miss this fact.

There are other little fees that can add up. Wire transfer fees, account statement fees, dividend check payment and legal document fees can add up over time. A good broker will post a clear and easy to understand fee schedule on their website and will also mention it in their terms of service agreement that you'll sign when you open an account.

If the quality of the broker's software is glitchy and regularly stalls, you'll need to phone in your trades. Most brokers charge a fee for this, and it can be as high as $25 per trade. Inactivity charges are another way that brokers will make money off you. This is especially the case with brokers who seek active traders as customers. If you're transferring your balance from one broker to another, make sure you know if transfer fees apply. Quality brokers will not charge you for the incoming transfer.

These are the primary features of a broker that you must consider before choosing one. These days it's quite easy to read reviews of brokers and to figure out what their customers are saying about them. Take special note of the negative reviews. Not all of them will be legitimate, but an unusual number of reviews that mention the same problem is a good sign of something wrong with that broker.

TWO BROKERS WE RECOMMEND FOR THE WHEEL STRATEGY

Note: We are not affiliated with either of the companies listed below, nor do we receive any commissions if you open an account with them. Brokers and fees change all the time, so be sure to double check before you open an account

- **Tastyworks by Tastytrade**
  - $1 per contract to open (capped at $10 per trade)
  - Cheaper fees for trading index options
  - Zero commissions to close
  - Can open/close both legs of the trade simultaneously
  - Easy to set up take automatic profit targets
  - Free ACH deposits & withdrawals
  - Excellent education platform
  - Available to European users
- **Thinkorswim by TD Ameritrade**
  - Commission free trading for US stocks & options
  - $0.65 per contract
  - No assignment fees
  - Easy to use software
  - US users only

"CAN I USE ROBINHOOD OR WEBULL FOR THIS?"

We get this question from email subscribers quite a lot, as many of them are using Robinhood or WeBull to buy stocks.

The answer is... yes, but we don't recommend it.

Newer app-based solutions such as Robinhood and WeBull are a decent starting point for investing, but they're poor choices to execute the wheel with.

For starters, it's far better if you use a computer screen to execute these setups. This extra step of "inconvenience" also promotes rational thinking and reduces your propensity to make impulsive decisions.

Combined with the fact that neither of these platforms has phone support if anything goes wrong (as you may have experienced with January's Gamestop fiasco) neither Robinhood nor WeBull is a good long term solution if you plan on executing The Wheel year round.

FREEMAN WHEEL STRATEGY RULE #2

YOUR CURRENT BROKER MAY NOT BE THE BEST CHOICE FOR OPTIONS TRADING

4

CHOOSING THE RIGHT CANDIDATES

Now that you understand how The Wheel works, it's time to look at the stocks you should focus on to execute this strategy. On the surface, the criteria for selecting the right stocks is simple. Choose stocks you'd be happy to own for the long term, or ones that you'd be happy to run a covered call on.

However, there are many nuances to this, and we'll be covering these in this chapter. Always remember these overarching criteria when you read this chapter. Don't get caught up in speculative forces that will push you to implement The Wheel on hot stocks or fast-moving ones. How happy will you be owning a stock over the long term, is the fundamental question.

Will you be happy owning AT&T at $28 or Bank of America at $24? That's what you should always ask yourself before committing to run The Wheel on specific stocks. As a rule of thumb, if a stock is a good covered call candidate, it's likely to be a good one to run The Wheel on. The Wheel is an income-generation strategy, but don't forget that price appreciation of the long stock will bring you the greatest gains over the long term.

If your focus is short term, then the premiums are what matter the most. You'll be better off writing options that are close to the money and capturing higher premiums in the process. When starting out, focus on your stock selection criteria more than anything else.

FREEMAN WHEEL STRATEGY RULE #3

THE BEST MOVE YOU CAN MAKE AS A WHEEL TRADER IS TO SELECT THE RIGHT STOCK IN THE FIRST PLACE

Selection Criteria

So what are the criteria you should look for? There are a few different elements. Let's begin by examining the state of the stock overall.

Trend Characteristics

For The Wheel to work well you need to look for stocks that are either moving sideways in a range or slightly upwards. Stay away from stocks that are declining. Note that there is a difference between a stock that is declining slightly and one that is in freefall. It's a good idea to examine the stock chart for evidence of support and resistance levels before entering the trade. If you see relatively stable support and resistance levels within which prices are moving, this is evidence of a range or sideways move. We'll be explaining support and resistance and covering examples of this in the next chapter.

Stocks that move sideways allow you to capture higher premiums. This is because you can write options that are close to the money without the added risk of them being assigned. IV levels will also be lower and this means your trade will live in a stable environment. Of course, sideways moves cannot be sustained for long. At some point, the stock will break out, upwards or downwards, at which point you'll need to either adjust your strikes or decide whether you want your puts assigned and buy the stock.

A sharply declining stock is a poor candidate even if you want to own the stock. The reason being, the capital losses you'll face will override the premium income you earn. It's best to allow the stock to decline to lower levels and target a strong support level from which you can initiate the trade.

A stock that is moving slightly upwards is a good candidate. However, note that these stocks can be more volatile and their IV numbers will reflect this. If you're happy owning it, consider writing your puts as close to the money as possible. If you'd like to earn additional income and enter when the uptrend is more defined, you can choose a strike that is further OTM.

If you aren't comfortable reading the price chart directly to determine what kind of a trend the stock is currently in, you can use indicators to help you figure this out. The ADX, for example, can help. This one is a trend strength indicator that fluctuates between 0 and 100, but it rarely hits those maximum values. Any number greater than 30 indicates a good trend, with numbers greater than 40 indicating a strong trend. Numbers below 30 indicate the absence of a trend. Good charting software will help you identify a stock's ADX value.

For The Wheel, you want to look for ADX numbers from 0 to 40, but if you're conservative, you can stick to values less than 30. Note that the ADX doesn't inform us about the direction of the trend, merely its strength. You'll need to look at the chart to figure out which way the stock is headed. A strong bearish trend will print the same numbers on the ADX as a strong bullish trend does.

You can also use moving averages and support/resistance analysis to help your evaluation of a stock's trend. We'll present some discussion and examples in the next chapter to help you better understand these analytics.

The internet is chock full of resources to help you grasp technical analysis and how to use it. If your grasp of the topic is weak, spend some time exploring the topic. Your trading results will improve as a result.

Stock Price

If your capital is low, you might be tempted to run The Wheel on low-priced or even penny stocks. The issue with this approach is that low-priced stocks are extremely volatile and are just as likely to rise by a huge amount as they are to fall to the same degree. If you recall from the previous section, you need to look at stocks that are in a moderate trend or are moving sideways.

These conditions almost never occur in stocks that are priced less than $5. If these stocks move sideways, it's because no one is trading them. Illiquidity is something you want to stay far away from. If the stock isn't being heavily traded, its options will suffer from even lower volumes. You'll find the premium spreads jumping all over the place and you'll have a hard time exiting your position.

By premium spread, we mean the difference between the bid and the ask. Typically you buy on the ask and sell on the bid. If the spread is wide, then, you may not get a price that makes the trade profitable. You'll find that the market in these low-priced stocks tends to be tilted towards one side. This means, even if the stock price rises, the spread just widens because the other side of the market isn't present.

This is why many low-priced stocks move violently in either direction. For example, buyers pump the stock up to high levels and once they wish to exit, they find that the bid remains low. This means they exit at low prices and the price chart prints a violent correction.

Another issue with these low-priced stocks is most of them aren't traded on reputable exchanges. They're traded on OTC markets for the most part and their options are equally unreliable. It's therefore best to stay far away from sub-$5 stocks. If you don't have the capital to trade stocks that are priced greater than this, then spend time acquiring enough capital to be able to do so. A lack of capital shouldn't push you towards trading unreliable stocks.

So how much capital do you need? With $2,000 you can trade one option of a stock that's priced at $20, with $5,000 you can trade an ETF priced at $50, and with $10,000 you can trade an ETF or a stock priced at $100. You might think there aren't many low priced stocks for you to trade. However, this isn't true.

Bank of America, FLIR Systems, Coca-Cola, AT&T, Intel and First Solar are examples of stocks that were good for people with smaller accounts in the past 2-3 years. With ETFs XLK (technology) and XLF (financials) were good candidates.

These instruments have been moving within the same price range for a long time now and are backed by decent fundamentals. This makes them great candidates for The Wheel. If you have access to a lot of capital, you can use it on higher priced stocks and ETFs like SPY & QQQ.

Stock Category

Well-known and recognized ETFs that are indexed. They could be indexed to a sector, an industry, or a popular market-tracking index. Whatever the underlying index is, make sure it's a nonvolatile one. The downside of participating in these ETFs is that they're often highly priced. However, we've highlighted a few exceptional ETFs that are moderately priced.

Look for ETFs that have been operational for at least 10 years and have a steady record of management. There shouldn't have been any mass chopping and changing of managers and the ETF should have posted returns closely in line with its index. The expense ratio should also be lower than 0.6% for a sector or thematic ETF and lower than 0.1% for a broad market or index ETF. Anything above this indicates fancy strategies that you ought to stay away from.

The assets under management (AUM) should be greater than $1 billion. This might sound like a lot of money, but for a reputable ETF with a good managerial team, it's pretty small. Most high-quality ETFs manage over $10 billion or more. Think of the AUM as being the same as the stock price of a company. The greater it is, the better.

No IPOs

We could extend this piece of advice even for investment purposes as well. Stay away from IPOs, even if you believe the company in question is a slam dunk. As we'll explain shortly, a slam dunk is one of the worst candidates for The Wheel. The problem with IPOs is that they tend to be extremely volatile. Everyone in the market wants a piece of the action and the stock promoter wants to get as high a price for their stock as possible.

Remember that companies raise cash from IPOs. For this reason, IPO prices tend to be inflated. As the market recognizes what's going on, violent corrections are possible. This is why the implied volatility of IPO stocks tends to be quite high. While volatility will help you on occasion, relying on it to produce consistent results isn't an intelligent decision.

Often, investors jump into IPOs because they buy the hype surrounding these companies. Stay well away from them and you'll do yourself a huge favor.

Stick to Boring Companies

High-growth companies are stock market darlings because they deliver astronomical returns quicker than a regular company's stock does. A portfolio of one or two high-growth stocks should be more than enough for you to be able to retire comfortably. For example, anyone who bought Amazon back in 2011 or earlier is probably sitting on a decent nest egg right now. Apple is also an example of a high-growth stock.

You'd think that capturing income as well as large capital gains will boost an already lucrative investment, and therefore The Wheel would be well suited for these companies. However, when you try to execute The Wheel on these stocks in real life, you'll find yourself leaving a ton of money on the table.

Thanks to the rapid appreciation that these company's stocks can undergo, your CSP is unlikely to move ITM. This means you won't be buying the stock. Even if you do manage to buy it, there's the problem of selecting a CC's strike price. If your CC finishes in the money and the stock is called away, you've capped your profit, thereby limiting your upside gains on these stocks.

Remember that the stock leg is the primary driver of gains. The option legs provide you with income that augments these primary gains. If a growth stock is primed to rise by 100% annually, it doesn't make sense to give this up in exchange for income that amounts to a one or two percent gain.

This theory was put to the test on Apple's stock by quantitative research firm Spintwig ("AAPL Short Put 45 DTE Cash-Secured Options Backtest," 2019). As a part of this backtest, 31,700 trades were placed on Apple over a 10-year period from 2008 to 2018. The options that were written in this test had an average expiration range of 45 days. This meant the strategy captured time decay in its entirety. This is another way of saying that the option premiums were maximized.

Positions in this backtest were managed early and often to adjust for optimum strike prices and this increased the average daily P/L per position from twice to 3.67x. The results of this backtest were great.

However, when the results were compared to a simple buy and hold strategy on the stock over the same time period, the options strategy underperformed massively.

This is because the rise in Apple's stock price was astronomical. There's no way option premiums can ever make up for a fast-rising stock price. This is why we counsel against operating The Wheel on stocks that you believe are likely to be home runs. If you spot any stock that you believe will be the next Apple or Amazon, then it's best to buy it outright and hold on to it for as long as possible. Don't bother writing options on it and risk it being taken from you during exercise.

You don't want to give up your long position in exchange for a few points in premiums. When viewed from a convenience perspective, it's hard to see why you would want to write options on these stocks. You'll have to spend time worrying about losing a good position and have to constantly watch out for vertical moves in the stock that could move your calls ITM.

It's better to stick to boring stocks that don't move much and won't give you sleepless nights. Going back to our earlier baseball analogy, don't bother trying to hit home runs. Stick to hitting singles and doubles instead. You'll compound these gains more reliably over the long term. If you hit upon a high-growth stock, buy it and plan to hold it long term.

To really drive the point home, let's answer the question one of our readers put to us recently: Is implementing The Wheel on Amazon stock a good idea or not. We say it's not a good idea, and recommended a buy and hold strategy for the following reasons.

First, to buy 100 shares of Amazon, the reader would need $320,000 in cash. This amount secures the CSP. There's also the fact that premiums on Amazon options are quite low. You're not going to earn much. Even with a 0.3 Delta (we'll explain Deltas in a later chapter if you're not familiar with them) you're going to earn just 4% per month, if that. Add to this the time you'll need to spend monitoring the trade, in case your CC moves ITM, and the strategy is already looking like it isn't worth it.

Most damning of all, the opportunity cost of having over $300,000 locked in a single trade is enormous, unless your portfolio is worth more than $30 million. Your profit, from running The Wheel on Amazon, will yield around 40% annually. This is great and outstrips the 18% you can earn by running it on the SPY. (Note that this is using 2020 numbers, so it is an analysis of the past - not a prediction.)

However in 2020, a simple buy and hold on Amazon yielded 73.5%, while a buy and hold approach on the SPY, on average, will yield 13%. The lesson here is that it's worth running The Wheel on the SPY, if you have the cash, but on Amazon you're simply creating more headaches for yourself by limiting your upside potential.

One way to mitigate this temptation is to apply a 1% dividend yield filter when screening for potential stocks. This will remove all growth stocks from your final list.

No Media Darlings

The financial media loves talking up certain companies as the "next Apple/Amazon/Facebook," etc. Often new sectors spring to life and this leads to a gold rush within those stocks. Over the previous decade, sectors such as marijuana and electric vehicles boomed and made some investors a fortune. However, we're willing to bet there were a greater number of investors who lost money in these companies.

Marijuana was the first darling of the decade. With promises of alternative medicine and the scientific proof that established cannabis and cannabinoids as legitimate healing methods, many companies rushed into the field once it was legalized. There were secondary effects of this boom as well. Virtually everyone who could grow marijuana became a "farmer" and sought to cash in on the boom.

In the stock market, companies that operated so-called weed farms became hot and zoomed in value. A few years later, most of these companies fell right back down because the economics of the sector didn't support valuations. We're not saying you shouldn't invest in this sector. It's just that every company that the media hypes ends up being a terrible long-term investment.

Media hype fuels price rises because everyone jumps into the stock. The electric vehicle sector is a good case in point. Tesla has been the flag-bearer for EV companies for a long time now. Many of its competitors have gone bankrupt trying to make the terrible economics of the sector work for them. However, thanks to smart capital raising, Tesla has operated like a tech startup, burning cash all the time, hoping to gain enough customers to buy their vehicles.

Other EV companies have jumped into the fray, using Special Purpose Acquisition Companies or SPACs to avoid having to go through the IPO process and the scrutiny that comes with it. Many Chinese companies that used to manufacture CDs are now EV makers. A graduate in mechanical engineering from Carnegie Mellon University founded an EV company and became a billionaire despite laughable revenue projections and zero technology.

Our point is that these hot sectors eventually come crashing back down. You'll be left holding the bag when this happens and your option premium income isn't going to be of any consolation. If capital gains are the primary profit driver, then capital losses are the primary loss driver. The quality of the company whose stock you're planning on holding matters more than anything else.

Some of the things to watch out for are companies that are dubbed the "next [insert favorite stock]". This kind of marketing panders to the get-rich-quick crowd that doesn't bother researching the companies they put their money into. Follow them and you'll receive their results. The next thing to look out for is a company that is clearly cashing in on the speculative hype around it.

The other kind of media darling to watch out for is the institutional darling. These companies are favored by large hedge funds and find themselves in the news because some money manager goes on air and starts talking about it. We're not saying that their motives are malicious. However, these companies always see a boost in their stock price in the short term before settling down.

Ultimately, all the media does is increase volatility in a stock. Because high volatility is your enemy when implementing The Wheel, you want to stay as far away as possible from it. Pick boring stocks that have boring businesses and you'll earn steady returns from them through their option premiums. With high-growth companies, such as Amazon or Apple, buy their stocks outright and don't bother with generating income from their options.

No Penny Stocks

We've already mentioned that the stocks you select need to trade for at least $5, or maybe even $10. However, we'll make special mention of penny stocks because many novice investors tend to be tempted by them at some point. Penny stocks are a bad idea no matter which angle you examine them from.

The standard narrative around a penny stock investment is that you can buy a stock for a few cents and see it rise to a few dollars. This rise will give you a four-digit return (in percentage terms). Gaining this much in blue chip stocks is impossible. After all, even a 100% rise in Amazon would put its stock price at around $6,500. The other factor to consider is that Amazon is already a trillion-dollar company. Doubling this is a considerable task.

Penny stock companies are typically worth a few hundred million or less. It's easier for a company to double a market cap of $100 million or less. This situation attracts many fortune hunters. However, despite their wish to act like investors, everyone ends up behaving like a speculator. The volatility in penny stocks forces them to behave like this.

Swings of 50% or more over a week aren't uncommon in penny stocks. Consider that a stock that sells for 50 cents has moved by 100% if it sells for a dollar. The numerical price doesn't seem too much, but its effect on your portfolio will be substantial. Many investors lose their nerve and end up trying to time their entries and exits. Even worse, some traders use leverage to boost their returns. What happens instead is that they lose their shirts.

Volatility is the reason you should stay away from penny stocks. Most of these stocks don't have active disclosure requirements because they aren't listed on the stock exchange. As we mentioned previously, they trade over the counter and their volumes are minimal. You'll be operating against company insiders who don't have insider trader laws to worry about. It's a lose-lose situation for you no matter which way you cut it.

You'll read many stories from trading gurus about how they turned a few thousands into millions using penny stocks. Some of them might even be former "hedge fund" principals. Take these stories with a truckload of salt. When former hedge fund managers sell courses to make a living, they were probably not very good at what they did.

So stay away from anything to do with penny stocks or the people who push them.

Specialty ETFs

Leveraged ETFs are the penny stocks of the investment fund world. We briefly mentioned these previously, but it's time to dive deeper into them. There are different kinds of leveraged ETFs you'll find in the markets. The first kind are the plain vanilla leveraged ETFs. TQQQ and TNA are examples of this category.

TQQQ aims to earn three times the returns of any movement on the NASDAQ. If the NASDAQ moves by a point, TQQQ moves by three. The way it does this is by borrowing money, thereby leveraging itself. TNA aims to 3X small-cap stock index returns. Small-caps tend to outperform large-caps in the long run. However, they do so with greater volatility.

To 3X these returns sounds like a great idea on paper. After all, most indexes rise over the long term and it isn't as if the NASDAQ is going to disappear anytime soon. So why not buy and hold a leveraged ETF over that time period? The problem with this line of thinking is that it doesn't take volatility into account. You cannot hold on to something for the long term if short-term volatility forces you into a margin call caused by a market correction.

These ETFs haven't faced such a situation as yet, but it's not an implausible one. If the market dips, these ETFs dip by 3X thanks to leverage. That's the price you pay for investing in them. Devoting a small portion of your portfolio to them might be a good move, as long as you understand the risk, but when it comes to implementing The Wheel on these ETFs, you need to reconsider your choice.

Excessive volatility will push prices in unpredictable ways. You might find that your CSP is ITM for the large majority of the holding period, but it moves OTM at the last minute. Using The Wheel on volatile instruments is like riding a rollercoaster. It's great for a few short minutes, but no one wants to be on it for a long time.

There's another category of leveraged ETFs you should stay away from. These are inverse ETFS that move in the opposite direction from their underlying index. The way they do this is by assuming short positions in the index using options. Implementing The Wheel on these ETFs is a risky move. Effectively, you'll be opening an option position on another option.

A single option position leverages your investment considerably since you'll control 100 shares of the underlying. To double this exposure isn't a smart move. Add to this mix the inherent volatility that these ETFs have and you've created a very risky situation. Stay away from inverse ETFs.

Many ETFs track commodities, and these can seem like a good option. Commodity investing is a diverse field and there are many ways that ETF managers can track their underlying product. Some choose the plain vanilla way by tracking index prices. Others track it by buying stocks in companies that have exposure to the commodity. Then there are the adventurous ones who track prices by buying futures and speculating on prices.

These too are especially risky. USO, which aims to track oil prices, is a good example. This ETF derives its price by speculating on WTI futures. However, when oil prices went negative in 2020 thanks to the COVID-19 crisis, the managers of USO changed their strategy without any notice and this caused the ETF's price to plummet even as oil prices were rebounding.

Finally, we have ETFs that track volatility. UVXY is an example of this. This ETF derives its prices from the VIX and offers a direct path to betting on volatility. There are many problems with investing in such complicated ETFs. Volatility is a derivative of the market. It measures how fast prices are moving, not their direction.

To make an intelligent guess about volatility, you need to be able to read market conditions extremely well and this takes time. It certainly isn't something you can do if you have only a few hours per week to devote to market analysis. Expert institutional investors get volatility investing wrong, so it's unrealistic to assume you can figure it out by spending a few hours per week.

The lesson here is that commodity ETFs or ETFs that don't directly track a simple index of stocks are a risky bet. They're volatile, and as an investor, you're at the fund manager's mercy. There's no telling when they might change their approach and leave you holding the bag.

Implementing The Wheel on these ETFs adds another layer of derivatives onto the situation. There's no telling how prices will move, and adjusting your position is going to be extremely tricky. It's best to stay away from them altogether.

STOCK SCREENER CRITERIA

To make stock selection easier, we recommend using a stock screener to help you narrow down your investment choices. There are a number of screening tools and sites, ranging from free to extremely expensive.

Finviz is perhaps the best free stock screener out there because it allows you to input both fundamental and technical criteria. Based on what we've said thus far in this chapter, here is the criteria you can input into Finviz to find stocks which tick our required boxes. Try accessing Finviz.com now and follow along as we tell you exactly what filters to select. Near the top of the page, you should see a horizontal ribbon with the word "Screener" in it. Click on it and make sure "All" filters is selected.

Optionality

To execute The Wheel, we need stocks that we are eligible to write options on, so find the Option filter and make sure Optionable is selected.

Price

Next, we fix our price criteria. Let's focus on $10 per share. The maximum price depends on your capital, because you will need enough money in your account to buy 100 shares when you take assignment of your CSP. So if your capital is $5,000 then your maximum price per share is $50.

Volume

Next, you should stick to stocks and ETFs that are heavily traded. Choose an average daily volume of at least 200,000 shares - with the last session's ("Current volume") equal to or greater than this number. This will weed out all instruments that are thinly traded as well as the ones that had volume spikes distort the average volume.

Stability

Filtering out growth stocks is important. Add a filter for a one-percent dividend yield and you'll get rid of high-growth stocks. These companies rarely pay dividends, which is why this filter works. Note that it isn't perfect. You'll need to check your list to check whether there are any media darlings in there.

Bullish Trend

Another good filter has price greater than the 50 Exponential Moving Average. Your version of Finviz may only offer the simple moving average as a filter. That's fine – use it if necessary. By screening for stocks above the 50 moving average, you will be identifying stocks in moderate bull trends. Of course, any stock could swing downwards violently once you enter, but this is a risk you'll have to assume. Technical analysis will help to screen stocks, as well. We'll cover that in the next chapter.

No Upcoming Events

One of the most important filters you should include is requiring that there are no earnings announcements coming up over the next 30 days. For the Earnings Date filter, chose "Previous Week". Many beginner options traders fall into the trap of writing options during earnings week. The thought process is that earnings week implies higher volatility, which means greater IV levels. This boosts premiums and therefore writing a CSP is a good idea. However, higher IVs also imply a greater potential drop in prices, even if the earnings exceed expectations.

Earnings announcements usually are not a major mover of stock prices; the earnings expected are already factored into prices. This doesn't happen because of insider information. Instead, Wall Street analysts gain deep access into the company's inner workings and project an earnings rate that is in line with the company's internal expectations.

This number forms a "baseline" for companies to hit and you typically do not see earnings reported much below or above this number. Thus, stock prices normally reflect earnings projections and the news is built into the price. The Covid-19 crisis, however, has shown how earnings projections can be wrong, and how stock prices can move violently in reaction. Therefore, you are better avoiding the stock price fluctuation that can occur with earnings surprises.

ETFs have an advantage in this regard. There are no earnings to report even if the underlying stocks report earnings. If you're sticking to ETFs, you won't have to worry about applying this filter.

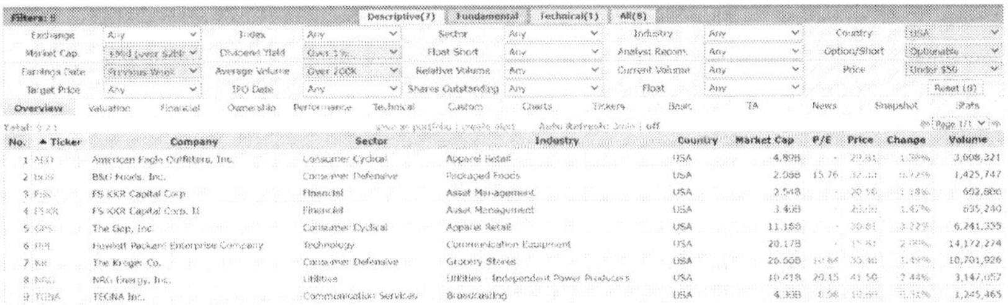

Figure 2: The Finviz screening criteria taken on March 14th 2021. As you can see, using the above criteria we have a selection of 8 stocks which would potentially be good candidates for The Wheel if your account size was less than $5,000.

We have also created a video tutorial of how to screen for stocks which would be good candidates for The Wheel on our YouTube channel. You can find the video at

https://freemanpublications.com/youtube

Paid Screening Tools

Aside from Finviz.com, you can use Barchart.com. The free version of barchart.com is quite robust, and the premium version contains a few criteria that are useful. The premium version costs $200 per year and allows you to screen stocks based on their IV level. IV is directly tied to option prices: the higher the IV, the higher the price of the option. As an option seller, we want to earn higher premiums, but doing so comes at a risk. The reason premiums are higher is because volatility is higher, and our stock has a potentially bigger range of movement during the option contract's lifespan.

Therefore when looking at IV level, we like to use the sweet spot of an IV between 30 and 50%.

So stay away from stocks like AMC that have a 408% IV number.

General Motors (40%), Twitter (39%), AMD (37%) Fox Corporation (36%), are more suitable Wheel candidates.

Barcharts premium version also allows you to select custom earnings dates, as Figure 3 illustrates.

Figure 3: Barchart.com Paid Screener

This concludes our look at the fundamental criteria for choosing stocks to implement The Wheel with. As you can see, they're quite straightforward, and they're extremely powerful. Not only are fundamental filters such as the ones we've highlighted, great, so are technical filters.

Technical analysis is often overlooked by long-term investors, but in our opinion, it has the potential to improve your ability to choose good candidates for The Wheel. The next chapter deals with technical analysis as it relates to screening stocks for The Wheel.

FREEMAN WHEEL STRATEGY RULE #4

USING STOCK SCREENERS CAN HELP YOU
RESEARCH GOOD CANDIDATES IN LESS TIME

5

TECHNICAL ANALYSIS FOR THE WHEEL (EASIER THAN YOU THINK)

Now that you have an idea of the kinds of stocks you should uncover with screeners, and the kind of broker you should use, it's time to get technical. Technical analysis (TA) of a stock is simply an examination of past price movement as documented on a chart. With today's sophisticated software, calculations of averages and standard deviations and other formula can be plotted on the chart, confusing the daylights out of you. We'll try to simplify by discussing just a few.

You probably know more about technical analysis than you realize. Did you understand the discussion on support and resistance in Chapter 3? If so, then you are well on your way. For you, then, some of the following is a review.

Recognizing Price Action Around Earnings

Earlier we mentioned that you need to be sensitive to the price action of your stock around earnings announcements and ex-dividend dates. By looking at a chart you will immediately be able to determine how the market has historically reacted.

The following chart from TradingView shows that the investment community was unhappy with IBM's earnings announcement in early 2021, but then reacted very favorably to the April 2021 announcement. The dates are clearly noted with a circled E at the bottom of the panel. "Big Blue" has become volatile in the past few years with the rise of more nimble players in the technology field.

You can also see that price tends to rise just before IBM's ex-dividend date. IBM's dividend of approximately 4.5% is considered exceptional and dividend "grab" trades drive up the price of the stock and then it drifts back down a bit.

Your broker's platform should provide charting capabilities that note these dates for the stocks you are evaluating.

Figure 4: IBM as an example of price plots with the candlestick technique, showing dividend and earnings dates. (Source: TradingView)

With a candlestick chart each day's trading record is shown as a rectangle with lines extending above and/or below. The rectangle is the "body" of the candle and is formed by the opening and closing prices for the day; the "wicks" are the lines extending above the rectangle, showing the high for the day, and "tails" are the lines below. Trading volume is presented at the bottom of the panel, in greyed-out colors. When a chart has long wicks or tails, traders take notice. A long wick, or group of wicks suggests selling, and if they appear on the chart after an upswing, traders expect a downturn. Likewise with tails, traders expect a change in price direction.

Support and Resistance

Areas of support, or resistance, are created when the forces of supply and demand for a stock suddenly change. Imagine a situation where a large investment firm has researched a biotech company and now wants to acquire tens of thousands of shares. The firm thinks this hot new company has a game changing medical solution, but wants the stock at less than $25 per share. If the firm were to go into the open market and start buying thousands of shares at once, that expansion of demand would drive up the market price.

The managers at the investment firm know this, so they issue instructions to their broker(s) to buy as many shares as possible but for no more than the $25/ share. As the orders are filled, supply of the stock at that price dwindles and the stock starts trading at higher prices. With the price increase, the firm's price limit curtails the buying, and demand decreases.

This ebb and flow can easily be seen on a stock's price chart. Let's look at two charts to see how areas of buying and selling interest become zones of support and resistance (S&R). Our first example is a daily chart of AT&T stock and charted on stockcharts.com

Figure 5: *AT&T price chart with support and resistance zones. (Source: Stockcharts.com)*

We've drawn horizontal lines to note the areas of S&R. The bottom line shows support – an area where changes in supply/demand forces turn the price direction back up. The top line, is the opposite – an area where the price advance is halted and buying interest in the stock diminishes. In our imaginary story of investment firm's buying interest, this chart suggests the broker might have instruction to buy if the stock trades around $27.50.

The wavy line is a 50 day moving average which started sloping upward in December of 2020. In the last chapter we included the 50 line as a screening criteria. You can see in AT&T's chart how the line helps identify stocks in uptrends when the criteria stipulates "greater than" the average. Since early March of 2021 the stock has been trading firmly above that line, which is bullish, but price is now close to that resistance line.

Will the resistance line hold again or will price break through this time?

No one can say from the limited information contained on this chart; and thus, many criticize technical analysis as backward looking, complaining that chart patterns are useless because they are recognizable only with hindsight. While this criticism has some justification, it is not totally founded. Institutions famously use moving average lines to determine entry or exit zones, and quite a few famous winners of stock-trading contests succeeded by using these technical indicators.

The fact is: When institutions become interested in acquiring a stock, they acquire LOTS of it, and that influx of interest will show up on a

TECHNICAL ANALYSIS FOR THE WHEEL (EASIER THAN YOU ... | 77

chart. Those who study charts will recognize the new interest, and they too will start acquiring the stock. Learn to read charts so that you, too, can recognize supply and demand forces.

Here's a monthly chart of Lennar from Yahoo Finance that demonstrates multiple S&R concepts.

Figure 6: Lennar's monthy price chart with support and resistance zones. (Source: Yahoo Finance)

First, notice how the longest horizontal line represents both support and resistance over time. One of the most telling features of S&R analysis is when a line is broken. The break signals a significant change in attitudes toward the value of the stock. In July of 2020, resistance was broken, and although selling put some downward pressure on price over the next several months, the $70 resistance zone became support, and the buying interest drove prices higher after the end of the year.

Notice, too, that the lines represent AREAS. Yahoo's technical analysis software declares support to be at $59.49, whereas we've drawn the line closer to $55. Do not fall into the trap of thinking S&R lines on a chart represent exact prices. They represent AREAS. The difference between the $59.59 and $55 is nothing to fret about.

Also notice the upsloping trend line drawn in 2020. The concept of S&R areas is not limited to a horizontal line; it applies to sloping lines as well.

The intersection of that upsloping line with the long horizontal line (around September of 2020) presents an interesting technical analysis conundrum –resistance was broken in July, 2020, but then the upsloping support was broken just a few weeks later in October. Which force will win this battle??! The astute trader waited until it was clear which side would win. Toward the end of the year, it became fairly certain that the $70 price zone would hold, and entries based on rising prices would likely be profitable.

Automatically adding Support & Resistance to your own analysis

If you're not comfortable drawing your own support and resistance lines, you can automatically add these to your TradingView account using a free plugin made by user *LonesomeTheBlue*.

You can add the plugin to your TradingView account by going to https://freemanpublications.com/SRplugin then scrolling down to the section beginning with "Want to use this script on a chart?"

Once you have added the plugin you can add support and resistance lines to any chart by using the Indicators tab on the chart page.

The thicker the horizontal bars, the strong the support or resistance level.

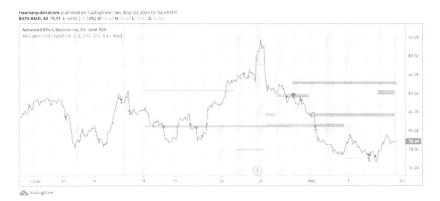

Figure 7: The monthly chart for AMD with the added support/resistance zones. The up or down arrows indicate when the support or resistance zone has been broken. (Source: TradingView)

Uptrending 50EMA and Bollinger Bands

Now let's look at other technical analysis tools. We've decided to demonstrate these to you using real Wheel strategy candidates we found on Finviz.com.

Using the same criteria we covered in the previous chapter, we found four trade scenarios to use as educational examples, these are not recommendations.

These charts were taken on December 18th 2020 and the passage of time invalidates viability. However, you can see how the right candidates can be selected or rejected.

Our first find is Hewlett Packard. The next page shows a one year daily chart with prices, trade volume, selected indicators and annotations. A discussion of those indicators follows the chart.

Potential Wheel Candidate #1: Hewlett Packard($HPE)

TECHNICAL ANALYSIS FOR THE WHEEL (EASIER THAN YOU ... | 81

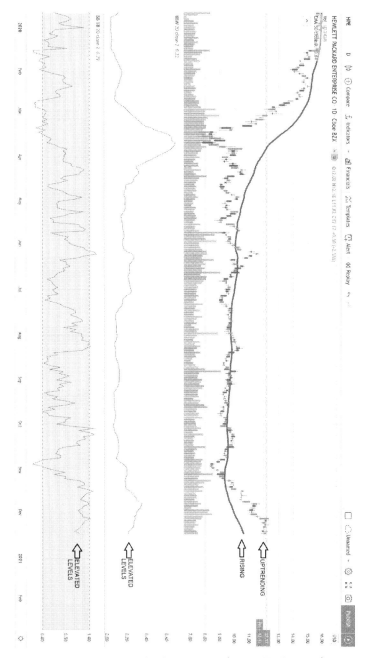

***Figure 8**: Hewlett Packard Price Action (source: TradingView)*

On the price section of the chart is a thick line that represents the 50-day Exponential Moving Average (50EMA) indicator. The 50EMA is used by institutional investors to determine the short-term trend of a stock. Notice the current price of Hewlett Packard is $12.17, which is above the rising 50EMA. The pattern of this stock's EMA line is one where a period of stability is followed by a recent turn upwards. (since November 2020) This uptrend suggests a higher probability of the stock price rising in the next 30-45 days.

Below the main price chart are the Bollinger Band Width and the Bollinger Band %B indicators. These two indicators are derived from the Bollinger Band indicator, which measures standard deviations from moving averages and provides the probability that a stock will enter either a trending phase or a consolidating phase.

Bollinger Bands, named for their creator John Bollinger, move like a rubber band. If the stock is trending (up or down), the bands stretch, with the Bollinger Band Width and %B indicators increasing in value. When the Bollinger Band Width and %B decline in value, that indicates a shift in stock price action, from trending to consolidating phase.

On this chart, the Bollinger Band Width is above .20, which is considered elevated levels, but not excessive. The Bollinger Band %B, is currently above .50, another indicator which demonstrates elevated levels. We have the probability that Hewlett Packard will be trading at higher prices in the next 30-45 days.

Hewlett Packard therefore is a good CSP writing candidate. Based on this chart, we think the price of HPE stock will increase in the next

30-45 days, and therefore we expect that we can run The Wheel and collect premiums as pure profit (less commissions, of course). The decisions to make will, of course, be strike prices and expiration dates, based on the premiums that the puts are yielding.

Spikes in Underlying's Price and Volume

The following chart shows the daily price action of SWBI (Smith and Wesson Brands). On the day this chart was captured, price popped above the flat 50EMA, and on relatively high trading volume. This is very bullish and the price of SWBI is expected to increase – an uptrend in both price and the EMA line should begin.

Potential Wheel Candidate #2: Smith & Wesson Brands ($SWBI)

84 | THE OPTIONS WHEEL STRATEGY

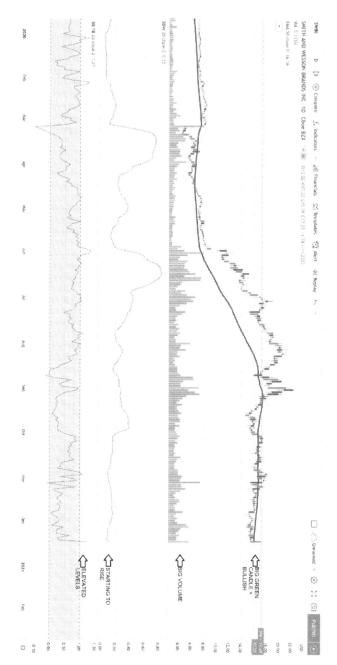

Figure 9: Smith and Wesson Brands Price Action (source: TradingView)

Smith & Wesson is a good cash secured put writing candidate, because the price of the stock will probably increase in the next 30-45 days. If we're interested in acquiring the stock, then we might write a CSP in the money, expecting assignment. Otherwise, a strike price below (OTM) the stock's current price presents the probability that the put call option we write will not be assigned, enabling us to collect premiums as pure profit (less commissions, of course).

MACD and RSI

The vast number of technical indicators available makes analysis difficult. You'll find that there are so many indicators, they can actually contradict each other in their interpretations.

We offer just two more here to add to your arsenal. We recommend that you become fluent in several indicators and use them together.

MACD is an acronym for Moving Average Convergence/Divergence. It measures the relationship of two different moving averages.

RSI stands for Relative Strength Index and it measures the internal strength of a stock's price moves. We'll discuss interpretation using the examples on the next pages, starting with the MACD.

Figure 10: *Kraft Heinz daily price chart with MACD lines graphed in lower panel. (source: Yahoo Finance)*

In this chart of KHC, as with all Price plus MACD charts, the lower graph has a straight horizontal line, called the "Zero line", and two oscillating lines, which are the moving average plots.

The upper graph presents the plot of daily prices. Notice how, in late December of 2020, the two MACD lines come together, with the more squiggly upper line ultimately crossing the smoother one, and then turning downward. This coming together of the lines happened while price was "consolidating" or moving relatively sideways. The MACD lines suggested the up move was over, and a downturn was due.

Figure 11: Intel's price chart with MACD lines graphed in lower panel.
(source: Yahoo Finance)

With Intel, price trended higher from mid-February until mid-April, 2021, while the two MACD lines wobbled down. The MACD lines were signaling a price correction was due. In other words, the upward price move was losing strength.

Figure 12: WMT's daily prices plotted with RSI shown in lower panel.
(source: Yahoo Finance)

Here is WalMart's price action in early 2021 with its RSI plotted. Again, you will need to expand your understanding of this indicator by doing some basic research on the internet. We're presenting just one use to start you on your way. Notice that there are two horizontal lines in the RSI graph – one at 70 and the other at 30. These often signal "overbought" and "oversold" conditions where a stock's price needs to take a breather. Here, in late February and early March, 2021, WMT's price had been declining, and the RSI crossed the 30 line. Not many days later, price reversed course, and the RSI line moved back into "neutral".

Note that RSI and the ADX indicator (discussed in Chapter 4) are similar in that they both measure strength. Many traders use them together, which brings us to our words of caution: **Don't pick one indicator and ignore the others.** If one gives you a good signal, look for confirmation from at least one of the others. Frequently you won't get a strong signal, and that's fine, but you do need to monitor these tools, looking for those times when a signal is flashing.

Now let's look at a couple of examples where Bollinger Band analysis is telling you to find another trade.

Stock Chart Pattern to Avoid #1: Designer Brands ($DBI)

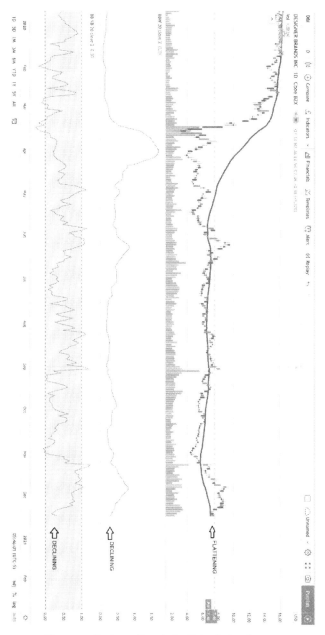

Figure 13: Designer Brands Inc Price Action (source: TradingView)

This chart shows the daily price action of DBI (Designer Brands). The current price of $7.46, is above the 50EMA, which is bullish, but the 50EMA is flattening. This gives us the probability that the current price of DBI will be trading within the $6.00-8.00 range.

The Bollinger Band Width is below .50, and it is currently declining, which gives us the probability that DBI will stay in the $6.00-8.00 range. The Bollinger Band %B is currently declining, which also gives us the probability that DBI will stay in the $6.00-8.00 range.

DBI is not a good CSP candidate at this time, because the price of DBI has a probability of going below the $6.00-8.00 trading range. A drop below that range means the CSP goes deep in-the-money, and more money would be lost on the long stock than the amount collected with option premiums.

With The Wheel strategy, we prefer to select uptrending stocks compared to consolidating stocks, so the chances of the options being deep in-the-money upon expiration date is very slim.

Stock Chart Pattern to Avoid #2: Golub Capital ($GBDC)

Figure 14: Golub Capital Price Action (Source: TradingView)

This chart shows the price action of GBDC (Golub Capital BDC). The current price of GBDC is $13.82, which is currently above the 50EMA, and the 50EMA currently flattening. This gives us the probability that the current price of GBDC will be trading within the $12.50-14.50 range.

The Bollinger Band Width is below .20, and it is currently flattening, which gives us the probability that GBDC will stay in the $12.50-14.50 range. The Bollinger Band %B is currently flattening, which also gives us the probability that GBDC will stay in the $12.50-14.50 range.

GBDC is not a good cash secured put writing candidate at this time, since the price of GBDC has a probability that it could go below the $12.50-14.50 trading range, which could make the put options written in-the-money, thereby losing more money than the premiums collected.

It is better to select uptrending stocks compared to consolidating stocks, so the chances of written put options being in-the-money upon expiration date is very slim.

Freeman Wheel Strategy Rule #5

It is better to master 2-3 technical indicators than have a broad knowledge of 50

6

HOW NEWER OPTIONS TRADERS LOSE THEIR SHIRTS - WATCH OUT FOR THE VIX

Every option trader out there knows and fears the VIX. The VIX is the volatility index and it measures the degree of volatility in the S&P 500. The index represents the volatility outlook for the next 30 days in the S&P 500 and measures this by gathering the IV of individual SPX options. In short, it's the market's view of volatility for the next month.

Many beginners to The Wheel have issues dealing with the effects that the VIX has on their positions. Let's look at this in more detail.

UNDERSTANDING THE VIX

There's a lot of material out there written about the VIX, but we'll keep it short. Volatility in the markets cuts both ways. If the market is rising sharply, the VIX will rise. If the market falls sharply, the VIX will rise as well. The only scenario in which the VIX falls is when market action is smooth and sustained.

A good proxy for estimating how the VIX will behave following an event is to ask whether market participants expected it or not. Let's take the example of the COVID-19 lockdowns on the overall market. While the rest of the world was busy locking down, trying to contain the virus, America was busy denying it even existed. As reality hit, lockdowns were initiated on an emergency basis and suddenly, everyone was locked in.

Figure 15 illustrates how the market behaved and the VIX's reaction to it.

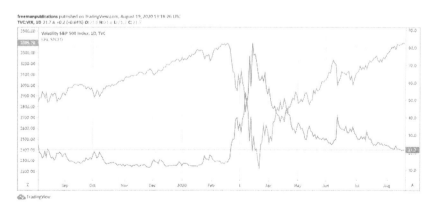

Figure 15: *The correlation between the VIX and the S&P 500 between September 2019 and September 2020 (source: TradingView)*

You can see that as the market crashed in early 2020, the VIX spiked. This led many traders to think that the VIX and the broad market are inversely correlated. When one goes up, the other goes down. This is only partially true. A more accurate representation is that the VIX doesn't have any direct correlation with the price action in the S&P 500. Instead it is correlated to the emotion connected to price moves.

The COVID lockdowns were unexpected because they were swift. As uncertainty about how the world would deal with this situation rose, the VIX rose as well. Note that as the market rebounded, the VIX settled down and fell back to normal levels. This is because the uptrend reassured everyone that everything was going to be normal and that the government was doing everything it could to support businesses.

Despite our assertion that you shouldn't correlate the VIX's movements with highs or lows in the S&P 500, we will admit that the VIX reacts far more sharply to bear runs than bull runs. This is because market participants don't like the pain that bear markets bring. This leads to excess emotion in the markets and the VIX spikes.

If you see the VIX spiking, make sure you check the S&P 500's price action before initiating a trade instead of automatically assuming you should go long. Even before you initiate The Wheel on a stock, make it a point to check the VIX.

VIX Values for The Wheel

For the VIX to be effective, we need a steadily moving market that's either meandering upwards or downwards. A market that's spiking all over the place isn't ideal. It's possible that you'll be able to unearth gently moving stocks in a volatile market. However, the overall market situation eventually spreads to all stocks within it.

Therefore, stay away from executing The Wheel when the VIX is greater than 30. Any value greater than this indicates a very volatile market, and you never know if that volatility could spread to your stocks, even if their Implied Volatility (IV) is low. This happens because of the way traders behave.

The broad stock market is composed of individual sectors. As the market rises upwards, certain sectors assume the lead and outperform the market while others underperform it. In the current bull run, tech and healthcare stocks have outperformed the broad market indexes. Infrastructure and retail stocks have underperformed and even lagged. Financial stocks have posted in-between performance.

As the bull run continues, different sectors take turns fueling it. This is because traders like to squeeze out every last drop of the bull run before turning bearish. Once the bull run in tech stocks becomes saturated, they turn their attention elsewhere, and in this manner, the bull run eventually affects every sector in the market.

Bear trends in the broad market begin with a once leading sector flagging and dropping off. The malaise spreads to every sector in this manner and before you know it, a full-fledged bear run is on. This is why you should be wary of the VIX. Overall market volatility might seem distant from your individual stocks, but it will eventually come to visit it.

As the volatility rises in the stocks you're following, you'll find that the option premiums will increase due to IV increasing. Beginners to

The Wheel will think this is good news. However, increased IV cuts both ways, as we've repeatedly mentioned thus far. Your options are just as likely to finish OTM as they are to finish ITM.

Therefore, stick to stocks with an IV between 30 and 50% and until you have a great deal of experience with the wheel, avoid entering trades when the VIX is above 30.

Freeman Wheel Strategy Rule #6

Avoid entering trades if the VIX is above 30

7

GREEKS FOR THE WHEEL IN 15 MINUTES

Options Greeks have a reputation for being tough to comprehend, but they are merely fancy labels for factors that influence an option's price. These factors should make sense to you. Time, for example, is one factor. Will the option expire in a month or a year? Wouldn't you expect to pay more for that year-long one? The Greek for time attempts to measure that effect.

Most beginners to options investing tend to seek strategies that don't require thorough knowledge of them. It IS possible to implement The Wheel without knowing anything about the Greeks, but in our opinion, you'll miss out on a wealth of information if you choose to do this.

Something to note about Greeks: they're derived values. These numbers are calculated using complicated option pricing models. As a result, the output is only as good as the input. You should keep in mind that during highly volatile moments in the market, especially during black swan events, these numbers don't always make sense, and can change minute to minute.

Therefore, always keep an eye on the VIX's behavior. If it's behaving erratically with sharp spikes, it's best to ignore the Greeks for The Wheel strategies; but remember our caveat stated in the previous chapter: avoid trading The Wheel when the VIX is above 30.

There are 5 factors that options traders evaluate the most, and we're going to discuss just two of them, using their Greek names: delta and theta. These measure the effect of the proximity of the option's strike price to the stock's price (delta) and the length of time remaining before the option expires (theta). Let's look at delta first.

DELTA

Delta measures the degree of movement in an option's premium, given a dollar's move in the underlying price. For example, let's say you've bought a call on Amazon. If Amazon's price rises by a dollar, and your call's premium increases by 25 cents, then the call option's delta is 0.25 or "25 delta". You can find delta values for any given optionable stock in your broker's option chain display. If you were to look at that chain right now, you would see that the delta of one option is different from that of another, and their values will all be different for a different stock.

Delta is a great measure of the relationship between the option's premium and the underlying price. An option's delta changes as time moves on and as the stock's price changes. An ATM option has a delta of 0.5 – the market's pricing of the option indicates that there's as much chance of an up move as there is a down move in the underlying stock's price. As the strike price moves further away from the underlying's price, the delta becomes smaller; and vice versa. Deep ITM options will have high delta values.

Probability

Option sellers, which is what you will be when you execute The Wheel, use delta very differently from option buyers. Sellers are primarily concerned with figuring out whether an option will finish ITM. Delta offers a great proxy for measuring how likely this is. An option with a delta of 0.5 has a 50% chance of finishing ITM. By reading the delta value as a percentage, option writers have an easy way of figuring out their chances of success.

Note that put deltas will always have negative values. This is because the value of a put rises as the stock price falls. You'll usually see deltas quoted on the basis of their absolute values. However, some platforms will display put deltas with the negative sign.

Remember that delta values depend on the underlying price's distance from the strike price. As the underlying's price gets closer to the strike price, the delta will increase. In the case of a put, the delta increases as the stock price decreases, bringing it closer to the strike. The opposite is true for a call where the underlying price must increase to move an OTM call ITM. Options that are either ITM or ATM will have deltas between 0.5 and 1. A delta of one indicates that the option has a 100% chance of finishing ITM.

Delta changes at different rates and from minute to minute, and from day to day, as do all of the Greeks. For example, an ITM option will see its deltas change faster than a deep OTM option. Let us say a call expiring next week is ITM with the strike price of $100 and the underlying price at $110. This option will have a delta close to 0.8 or even 0.9. After all, it's expiring next week and the chances of it moving OTM are decreasing as time passes.

A call that is expiring in 60 days will have a delta closer to 0.5. This is because there's more time left for the option to move OTM, and the Theta factor (discussed next) is pulling on the delta one. The closer you get to expiry, the more certainty there is and therefore deltas reflect probabilities more accurately. An OTM option will see its deltas decline steeply the closer it gets to expiry. The exception is ATM options. Their deltas will remain at or near 0.5 as they inch closer to expiry.

Volatility also plays an important role in determining option deltas. The greater the option's IV is, the more likely it is that its delta will hover around 0.5. This is because the high IV makes it probable that the option will finish OTM even if it's currently ITM.

THETA

Options are time-bound instruments, which means their value depends on the time left until expiration. As the option comes closer to its expiration date, its value decreases. It's easy to understand this intuitively. However, what if there was a way to measure the rate at which the option's value decreases, as time passes? Enter theta.

Theta measures the effect of time decay on an option. It can be found near delta in the option chain listing and is usually shown as a negative number. This is because it has a negative effect on the option premium. For example, if a call has a listed premium of $5.25 and a theta of -0.1, its time value portion of the price is going to decrease by .1 the next day. If the other Greeks are held constant, the option's premium will therefore be $5.15.

Theta doesn't decay at a constant rate throughout the option's lifecycle. As the option moves towards its expiration date, especially in the last 30 days of its life, theta decay accelerates. When you write an option, you are "shorting" and time decay is good for a short – you want it to decay in value so that it will expire worthless, or when you roll it into another option, you'll be buying back the option for less than your premium received.

This is why we've repeatedly mentioned that it's best to write options that have between 30 and 45 days until expiration. By doing this you'll capture the maximum premium possible before it starts declining. There's a huge advantage to capturing theta decay like this. If your position doesn't work out in your favor, you can cover your short and still capture some profit.

Theta Curves

The theta curve is the rate at which an option's theta changes as it moves closer to expiry. Here's where things can get confusing. Not all options have the same rate of theta decay. Depending on where they are relative to the money, theta decay can accelerate as far as 40-50 days out instead of in the final month.

For example, deep OTM options decay the fastest when they're 40-50 days out from expiration. This is because these options are used as insurance to hedge portfolio positions. As they move closer to the expiry date, their premiums stop decreasing. However, options that are closer to the money don't behave this way.

So what are the implications of this when you set up The Wheel? If you're planning on writing options that are significantly OTM, the premium will be a lot smaller than for those closer to the money. Therefore you should select options that are 60 days out from expiration, instead of 30 days. Generally speaking, though, it's best to avoid all this complexity and choose options that are close to the money.

There's another issue you should remember. The Greeks provide an approximate method to explain the price of an option. They are derivatives and are tough to measure. You'll often see theta-to-premium relationships go haywire when expiration is close. Often, theta will imply a negative option premium, but this is unrealistic. Therefore, it's best to choose underlying stocks that aren't very volatile and make reasonably predictable moves.

If you've been following everything thus far, you'll be wondering how theta behaves over the weekend. If theta declines constantly, then surely selling options on Friday and buying them back on Monday is a foolproof strategy? The market will be closed on the weekend and you can collect the days of theta for free.

In theory this is correct. Theta will decline no matter what. However, the people on the other side of your trades aren't beginners. They're market-makers and happen to be the most sophisticated operators in the market. They are well aware of the risk of theta decay over the weekend and don't want to be buying premiums heading into it, nor can they decline to trade since market rules prohibit them from doing so.

What they do instead is adjust volatility. (The Greek term is Vega.) They decrease volatility headed into the weekend, which lowers the option premium. Once Monday arrives, they increase volatility and the option's premium reflects just one day's (Monday) worth of theta decay instead of three (Saturday, Sunday, and Monday). Thus, this strategy is invalidated. Volatility is adjusted by widening the bid/ask spread and changing quantities that they trade in the market. It's a sophisticated operation

Should you avoid opening new positions on Friday then? Not quite. The market is designed to function as smoothly as possible, so it's not as if you'll face disruptions. The lesson here is that volatility (Vega) can negate the effects of theta. If volatility decreases significantly, theta decay's impact on the option's price can be minimized. However, it isn't a directly proportional relationship. It depends on where your option is relative to the money. A close to the money option that experiences volatility will likely overcome theta decay and the premium might remain the same or increase. This is why it's best to steer clear of volatility and keep an eye on the VIX. Larger market events can disrupt your investment thesis by introducing volatility at the wrong time.

To summarize, pay attention to options deltas and maximize theta decay by writing close to the money options that are 30-45 days away from expiry. Remember that these numbers are approximations and that volatility can introduce chaos into your plans at any moment, so you DO need to monitor your options positions.

You can trade very short time frames, which is what weekly options represent, but understand that you'll have minimal theta decay. Your account will have greater turnover and you can make more money. However, this is a more active method of investment. Our recommendation is to stay away from weekly options because of this and to instead look for passive income generation by writing options that have at least 30 days to expiry.

FREEMAN WHEEL STRATEGY RULE #7

ENTER TRADES WITH 30-45 DAYS LEFT
UNTIL EXPIRY

8

EXECUTING THE WHEEL STRATEGY: PUTTING IT ALL TOGETHER

Executing The Wheel is quite straightforward but depends on your investment objectives. If your position is a short-term one and if you aren't looking to own the stock for a long time, then avoiding assignment is the best way forward. If long-term investment is your objective, then assignment shouldn't worry you. In fact, if long-term investment is your goal, it's hard to see how The Wheel can negatively impact you.

In that scenario, if you're not assigned the stock, you keep the premium. If you're assigned the stock, you're now long a stock you want to own and, on top of that, you got paid to enter the market.

Let's review.

THE FIRST STEP

You need to screen candidates and find suitable stocks to initiate the trade. Remember to follow the criteria we listed in Chapter 4. Your aim is to find good stocks that have a good premium, not just stocks that have overpriced premiums. Generally these will be stocks with an IV of between 30-50%.

As a numerical rule of thumb for premiums, you want to look for stocks whose premium is at least one percent of the stock price. For example, if the stock is selling for $30, you want the premium to be 30 cents.

Based on what we've noticed over the years, most investors will find a handful of stocks that they like and have good premiums attached to them. You don't need a vast portfolio of stocks to make The Wheel work. Select a few and get to work.

Figuring out your capital requirements is the next step to take. You'll need to be able to buy at least 100 shares of the underlying stock. Figuring this out is simply multiplying price per share times number of shares. For example, if the stock is selling for $20, you'll need $2,000 (20*100) to execute the CSP. Remember that you should calculate the money you need based on the put's strike price. After all, this is the price at which you'll be assigned the stock.

When the time comes to enter the market, don't hesitate or try to time your entry. Pull the trigger and place the trade. Many traders try to time their market entries and end up missing the trade altogether. Many market professionals do advise AGAINST placing a trade during the first hour that markets are open. However, you shouldn't make the mistake of trying to optimize your entry for a few cents and end up missing the opportunity to make hundreds. Don't try to predict further dips or spikes. Once you've carried out all the analysis as we've detailed, enter and wait.

Keep your investment objectives in mind. If your aim is to get assigned, then write your CSP as close to the money as possible. You'll collect a large premium and the probability of your put being assigned will be high.

If you wish to avoid assignment, then stick to writing CSPs using the options with deltas around 0.3. This can be interpreted to mean there's a 30% chance of them being assigned (70% chance of being unassigned). Usually these options will be between 1-3 strikes OTM. See figure 16.

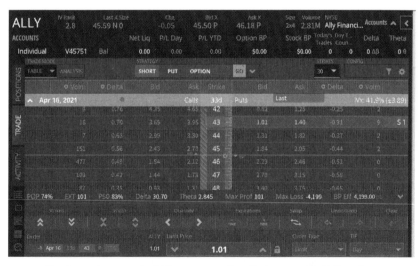

Figure 16: An example CSP entry point for Ally Financial (ALLY) with 33 days to expiry. The premium for the 2 strikes OTM 43 put at -0.31 delta fits our criteria of being at least 1% the price of the stock. In this case the premium is 2.21% ($1.01/45.59). (Source: Tastyworks)

While you can earn higher premiums by writing strikes closer to the money, this also means you have a greater likelihood of being assigned.

FREEMAN WHEEL STRATEGY RULE #8

ONLY ENTER THE TRADE IF THE OPTION PREMIUM IS AT LEAST 1% OF THE TOTAL STOCK PRICE

MONITORING THE CSP

You're now in the trade and will need to monitor it for a few minutes each day. Your trade will likely have a month to go until expiration. If you're operating using weekly options, your position will be more volatile and you'll have to spend more time monitoring it. Either way, at this step you'll have two possible scenarios.

The first is where you are not getting assigned. If your CSP looks like it will expire worthless, it will probably be best to roll the put and collect your next round of premium.

"Rolling" with many broker platforms is easy, as you can order the two legs simultaneously: close the old position and open a new one at a different expiration and/or strike price. If the stock has risen in price, you'll need to decide on a new strike price. A look at the stock's price chart with technical indicators can help. Remember to pay attention to the option deltas at that higher price. Again, stay as close to 0.3 delta as possible.

There's another situation in which you want to roll your position. If you don't want assignment and the stock moves too close to your CSP strike price, you can roll your position "down", buying back the original CSP for a certain price and opening a new CSP at a lower strike.

In this scenario, the roll may be for breakeven, where your buyback cost is the same as the premium collected on the new CSP. Frequently, though, you'll collect more premium than the buyback will cost you.

However, you may find yourself in a situation where the roll costs you to stay in the trade, and accepting assignment might be a better decision. You'll need to re-assess your view of the stock's prospects and evaluate the premium on calls to decide if you want to (a) take the small loss on the roll, planning to recoup that money with the next CSP; or (b) not roll the CSP and accept assignment, planning to sell a call against the shares.

We believe that the only situation where rolling for a slight loss is justified is when conditions in the stock have changed. Situations in the market are never constant, and rarely black and white, so you need to continually evaluate your trade.

The second scenario is where you opt for assignment and take ownership of the shares. Remember that it's 100 shares for every contract. These shares will now be in your brokerage account in the same way they would be if you had just bought the stock.

If your aim is to acquire and hold the stock for the long term, then there's no need for you to worry about rolling your CSP. After all, you'll gain ownership and you'll get to earn a premium through the CC leg of the trade. If you don't want a long term hold, then you can place the strike on the CC slightly ITM and get the bonus of earning a premium for selling a stock that you don't want to hold.

WRITING COVERED CALLS

Once you own the stock, the next step is to write a CC against it. Make sure you understand your broker's platform. Many brokers have a separate button for covered calls. Upon clicking this, the broker simultaneously buys 100 shares of the underlying and writes a short call against that position. However, you already have 100 shares of the underlying and don't want to buy more. Therefore, make sure you're only writing a call against your share ownership. For example, in Tastyworks make sure you select "Sell Call Option" rather than "Sell Covered Call." The broker will automatically use your shares when your order is filled.

When writing the CC, remember to use the same principles as when you wrote the CSP – write calls that have a delta of around 0.3 and are between 21-45 days out from expiry, if you wish to avoid assignment.

Choosing a strike price is a balancing act – the closer to ITM, the higher the premium, but also the smaller your gains on the long stock will be if your call is assigned. You need to know your overall objective in this trade. If you believe the stock has excellent long term prospects, you don't want to lose the stock for a small premium differential. Make sure you compare the premium you'll earn by writing a call close to the money versus writing another one further away. While the premium will be lower on the latter call, you'll make more through the capital gains you should see by holding a quality stock over the long term. Evaluate the trade-offs and choose a call strike price appropriately.

If you want assignment the process is much the same as it is with the CSP. Your broker will automatically sell your underlying holdings at the call's strike price and you can start The Wheel all over again with a CSP.

The worst-case scenario that can occur with a CC is that the stock declines in value. In this case, you'll have an unrealized loss on your stock with the CC premium mitigating it to a certain degree.

If your view is long-term, then letting the stock dip and rolling your CC downwards is a good decision. Or you could simply hold the initial CC until expiration and open another CC and keep capturing premiums.

What if the stock surges upwards and moves your CC ITM? In this case, you'll have captured a profit on the long stock plus the premium on the call. You will have to choose– accept assignment and then re-enter, or roll the call, or simply buy back the call and wait for the stock price to settle before writing another call.

The former scenario makes sense for those who wish to get out of their position planning a short term trade. If your aim is to hang on to the stock for the long term, then covering your CC is the smart move. You'll take a small loss on the CC position, but you can make up for this by writing another CC at a higher strike price. You'll maintain stock ownership and can partake in the increased capital gains.

One risk to consider in this situation is early assignment. Early assignment usually doesn't occur, but if it does, you'll lose stock ownership. However, it isn't as if you'll lose money. Your CC will be assigned and you'll sell the stock for a gain. You'll keep the premium from the CSP and CC, thereby boosting your overall profit. The only loss you'll face is that of opportunity cost. You won't get to take part in the capital gains if the stock continues to rise and you are not positioned. In the long run, this could slow the rate of your portfolio growth.

REPEAT

The last step is the simplest one. You simply repeat everything you did previously and initiate The Wheel once again. You can initiate a new Wheel on the same stock or find new candidates. We do not recommend a scattered approach where you are repeatedly writing puts on new candidates. Focus on a few good companies that you believe to have good long term prospects, and then use The Wheel to trade them again and again. You can use The Wheel to expand and contract your total holdings in a given stock.

When re-initiating The Wheel on an existing long-term investment, you'll again be faced with a choice. Remember the CSP will require you to have enough cash to buy 100 shares at once. If you don't have that cash, do you simply wait until you've saved enough, or do you start gradually acquire shares?

For example, let's say you first initiated The Wheel on a stock that was priced at $20. Over time its price has increased to $30, which is a great 50% gain. However, a new Wheel on this stock will require you to have at least $3,000 to write a CSP. What if you have just $1,500? Should you wait to gather more money, or should you buy as much as you can?

It depends on how quickly you can gather the remaining amount. For short-term investors, it's best to gather the money and then initiate The Wheel. You're not planning to own the stock for long, so it doesn't make sense to buy whenever you can. Also, monitor your portfolio allocations. Remember our advice in Chapter 1 – you should devote 15% to 25% to The Wheel, and the balance to other investment vehicles.

FREEMAN WHEEL STRATEGY RULE #9

ALWAYS STICK TO A DISCIPLINED MONEY MANAGEMENT STRATEGY

9

ADJUSTMENTS FOR SHORT-TERM INVESTORS

If you wish to execute The Wheel for a short-term investment, adjusting the trade is critical. This is because over the short term, avoiding assignment is the best move. The only situation in which assignment is a good scenario is if it helps you avoid a loss. There's no other reason for you to opt for it.

By holding on to the long stock, when that was not your original plan, you'll be locking your capital into a trade that may or may not pay off. You might think that the premium from the CC will compensate you for the lost CSP premiums, but this isn't always the case. If the stock is primed for a bearish run, the CC premiums will adjust downwards accordingly.

Therefore, rolling becomes all-important. Here are some tips that will help you roll your trades better and avoid assignment.

EARLY CLOSEOUT

Part of good trade management is learning when to close your trade. The objective is to gain the maximum profit possible, in as repeatable a manner as possible. The second half of that sentence is what many beginner traders and investors trip over. You might think that holding on to your trade until the very end will bring maximum profit, but this isn't true.

A backtest conducted by Spintwig found that closing a trade at 50% profit or at 21 days to expiry (whichever comes first) yielded the greatest profits ("SPY Short Put 45 DTE Cash-Secured Options Backtest," 2019). This seems counterintuitive at first, but it yields some interesting conclusions.

If you're closing your trade at the 21 days to expiration mark, your average holding period will be around nine to 24 days. Because most traders write CSPs at the 30 days to expiry mark, we can assume that a nine-day period is common. This is almost the same as the weekly options strategy.

We can conclude that a weekly options strategy is therefore the best choice for a short-term investor. You'll be able to place more trades, and despite your wins being smaller, you'll have more of them. Consider a trader who places three trades and makes $50 each, versus a trader who places one trade in the same period of time and earns $100.

While the latter's average win is higher, there's less money in total, compared to the former trader. A good example of this was Spintwig's

45-day backtest on AT&T stock ("T Short Put 45 DTE Cash-Secured Options Backtest," 2019). This backtest consisted of 30,000 trades and proved that a weekly Wheel strategy was the best.

Of course, if you're going to avoid assignment of the CSP, you'll rarely be initiating the CC portion of the trade. This is fine. The CSP premiums can produce the profits. The aforementioned backtest also highlighted that the weekly approach was 333% more effective in terms of capital management as opposed to holding all the way till expiry, because your capital is tied up for a much shorter period of time.

We're using the term "weekly" here to indicate the nine-day holding period. If you choose to implement this strategy with weekly options, your results will be better than when holding monthly options until expiry, but not as good as holding monthly options for nine days. Time decay plays an invaluable role in the process, and with weekly options you'll have already lost most option premium value.

AVOID ASSIGNMENT

We've mentioned it before, but it deserves mentioning again. For short-term investors, avoiding assignment is paramount. There's not much upside to this situation. Yes, you stand to gain on the long stock, but that's far from guaranteed. In fact, if the stock moved your CSP ITM, then the stock is most likely declining in the short term.

This means your money is going to be tied up in the strategy and you'll lose the ability to initiate new Wheels. The only reason for you to even consider assignment is if it helps you avoid a loss. If the stock you're looking at is due a bounce off a strong support level, then consider assignment. If not, it's best to cut your losses and cover your CSP.

If you're getting called more than three or four times in a year, then either the stocks you've selected are unsuited for The Wheel or you're mismanaging your positions. Getting assigned should be a rare occurrence for short-term investors. Your CSP leg will be the primary driver of profits.

BE RISK-AVERSE

When it comes to exiting options positions, it's always better to be risk-averse and close your position early than hold it all the way to expiration. We've already highlighted how closing your CSP with 21 days remaining is best. If the backtests didn't convince you, and if you don't want to deal with the additional monitoring activity that comes with small holding periods, then consider closing your position when you've captured 90% of the profit.

If you're terribly risk-averse, consider closing it out when you've captured 80% of profits. You won't capture maximum profits, but you'll be guaranteed a steady stream of income. Besides, you'll remove the possibility of anything adverse happening and pushing your option ITM.

This is especially the case if your position hits the 90% or 80% mark early in the expiry cycle. For example, if your option has declined by 80% within 10 days of opening the position, it doesn't make sense to hold one for another 20 days to collect an additional 20%. The option could move ITM in that time and you'll lose the profit.

So always close out early. This removes the risk of assignment and allows you to capture profit as much as possible. You can also free up your capital to initiate more trades. This means you can earn more money, even if you aren't capturing maximum profit all the time.

DON'T "SAVE" STOCK

This tip applies to the CC leg of The Wheel. Often, short-term investors will write the CC and see the underlying stock's price burst upwards, thereby putting the call ITM. This isn't bad—it's a profitable situation. However, the problem occurs if the stock continues to climb and greed sets in. When this happens to you, don't be tempted to just buy the stock outright. If your stock is called away and you feel it has further to go, write another CSP at a strike that you think will be assigned. You'll get the stock and the collect the premium on the put.

Focus on developing and executing a strategy that you can apply over and over again. In the long run, you'll make money and lots of it. Leave the greedy stock chasing to others.

DEALING WITH BLACK SWAN EVENTS

While we try to foresee all potential scenarios using the VIX and IV levels, it's best to accept that you'll deal with a black swan event at some point. Being prepared for worst-case scenarios is the best defense in today's markets. Long-term investors don't have to worry about black swan events, trusting that a quality stock's price will rise over their long term holding period.

Short-term investors have to be wary, though. From The Wheel's perspective, there isn't too much a black swan could do to you. Let's say the market crashes after you've initiated a CSP. You can either cover your position early or opt for assignment. As long as you've selected a quality stock, we recommend you take assignment. You'll keep the premium, own a good company, and be able to write calls. Those call premiums will be quite profitable because premiums will explode in value with the increased volatility that a market crash creates.

If the market rises sharply, you'll keep your premium as well. Either way, you're covered. The problem occurs for those trading on margin. This is why black swan events bring so much pain. They wreak havoc with those people who cannot afford to hold their investments thanks to borrowing too much money to buy them. It is these people who suffer the most.

Take care to never over-leverage yourself or chase easy money. Even in today's highly regulated markets, there are many instances of dubious companies listing themselves and positioning themselves as safe investments. Luckin Coffee, Nikola, and Aurora Cannabis are just a few recent examples.

History has many examples of fraudulent companies. Always carry out thorough research on the stocks you're looking to buy. Don't fall for promises of stock prices that can go through the roof. If you don't have the cash to write a CSP, don't borrow money to do so. It's better to save cash and then put it to use in the markets.

If you happen to have a position in a stock that crashes due to a black swan event, remain patient and don't sell; HOLD on to it. The famous line from the movie, *It's a Wonderful Life* is: "Potter's not selling!" If it's a good company and its underlying economics are sound, it's best to keep holding on or even buy more. You can execute The Wheel at these lower prices and reinvest the premiums into the stock. This will boost your returns dramatically.

An approach that some investors take is to invest in dividend stocks. This way, you open another income channel in your investment and this can soften the capital losses you'll suffer when a black swan event hits. However, don't make dividends the sole reason for investment. The quality of the business matters above all else.

If you entered the stock for the wrong reasons and cannot make a solid investment case for it, it's best to cut your losses and exit your position. This will be extremely painful to do, but it's the right way forward. Many people keep hanging on to their bad investments in the hope that they'll rise at some point, but this never happens.

All they end up doing is tying up their capital, missing opportunities to make their money back. So always cut your losses short, no matter how painful it might be. Most of all, do not ever use margin to fund The Wheel. Use cash at all times.

TRACKING PROFITS

Many people have trouble tracking profits when executing The Wheel. To help you with this, we're including a spreadsheet that will simplify profit tracking for you. Many so-called gurus charge you over $1,000 for their courses where items like this are available, but we're offering it to you without any strings attached.

To get your copy just go to

https://freemanpublications.com/wheeltracker and select File > Make a Copy

Note: Please do not request edit access, such requests will be ignored

The Wheel Strategy

Stock	AT&T		Ticker	T	
CREDITS					
Action	Date	# of Shares (1 contract = 100 shares)	Credit or Share Price	Total $ Received	Status
Sell CSP	4-Jan	100	0.40	$40.00	Closed
Sell CSP	10-Jan	100	0.37	$37.00	Closed
Sell CC	10-Feb	100	0.56	$56.00	Closed
Sell CC	24-Feb	100	0.55	$55.00	Closed
CC Assignment	3-Mar	100	29.00	$2,900.00	Closed

DEBITS				
Action	Date	# of Shares	Debit or Share Price	Total $ Paid
Buy-to-Close CSP	10-Jan	100.00	0.18	$18.00
Assigned CSP	8-Feb	100.00	28.00	$2,800.00
Buy-to-Close CC	24-Feb	100.00	0.22	$22.00

Figure 17: *The Wheel P&L Tracking Spreadsheet with an example run of The Wheel on AT&T (You should become accustomed to using the terms, "debits" and "credits". Simply think of this: Your broker "credits" your account when adding to it. A debit is a subtraction.)*

A single tab of this spreadsheet corresponds to a round of The Wheel. Once you move to the next round, move to the next tab. For example, here's how a sample round of the Wheel might go for you:

1. Sell CSP for premium - credit
2. Roll CSP - debits
3. Sell CSP - credit
4. Get assigned - debit
5. Sell CC - credit
6. Roll CC - debit
7. Sell CC
8. Get assigned - credit

Note that in every round you'll always have two more credits than debits. When calculating your profit, it's key to remember your cost basis. This is what our spreadsheet helps you do. If you choose to use other profit tracking methods, always remember to track your cost basis.

You can view a video tutorial for how to use this sheet by going to

https://freemanpublications.com/wheeltutorial

FREEMAN WHEEL STRATEGY RULE #10

REMEMBER TO ACCOUNT FOR COMMISSIONS WHEN TRACKING YOUR P&L

10

MONEY MANAGEMENT

As every successful investor will tell you, money management is what matters more than anything else. So how should you manage your money with The Wheel? It turns out it's quite simple. However, in the interest of completeness, we'll cover all aspects of money management in this chapter.

A lot of money management is psychological rather than anything related to your trades. Disciplined investors can lose their heads once they start making money and start ignoring rules. This leads them to open investments in poorly conceived ideas and the next thing you know, they've lost their accounts. Always remember that the suitability of the stock is what matters the most.

Everything else is secondary. The stock's option chain might give you the highest premiums, but if it's a stinker, no amount of premiums can make up for it. Short-term investors might argue that they're not looking to own the stock, but this ignores the worst-case scenario. If you're assigned the stock and it turns out to be a poor investment, those premiums aren't going to be of much use.

It takes many years of writing CCs to lower your cost basis to zero. Thinking your CCs will cover your poor investments isn't a viable strategy. Always focus on the quality of the stock using principles we've outlined in our other books.

CAPITAL NEEDED

All money management questions begin with figuring out how much money or capital you need to make The Wheel work. Our recommendation is to begin with at least $2,500. This will allow you to implement The Wheel with better quality stocks and ETFs.

While it's possible to trade stocks and ETFs priced below this, keep an eye out for sudden bursts of volatility. Remember that price alone shouldn't be your criteria when choosing a stock or ETF. As a rule of thumb, the cost of initiating the CSP should be less than 10% of your overall portfolio.

For example, if you're running The Wheel with AT&T priced at $29, the cost of initiating the CSP will be (29*100) $2,900. Your overall portfolio should be worth $29,000 or more to initiate this position. Why is this 10% threshold so important? In short, it helps you mitigate risk and manage any volatility that might occur within the position.

When trading options, volatility is always a concern and you shouldn't expose your broader portfolio to those swings. Keeping your Wheel position around 10% is a great way to mitigate this risk. The Wheel is a strategy that can be implemented over and over again. It isn't like a regular stock market investment where you buy a stock and then need to search for another idea all over again to put your money to work. The Wheel is immensely scalable and works no matter what your position size is.

The key to successful money management is minimizing risk. Profits take care of themselves as long as your strategy is good. Many investors sabotage great strategies by practicing poor money management. By limiting your Wheel position to 10%, you'll avoid this trap.

In the example we just highlighted with AT&T stock, it might seem as if ~$30,000 is a large number. What if you have a smaller amount of capital? If you have a small account, you can raise this threshold to 35%. Make sure to dial it back to 10% once you reach the $30,000 mark, though.

For example, if you have $7,500 in your account as capital, you can initiate a CSP worth $2,500. Keep decreasing the threshold as your account size increases. Remember, you need to hold cash in your account to make the CSP work. Holding 35% of $30,000 means you'll be holding over $10,000 as cash. That money can be put to work buying other stocks for the long haul or investing it in a dividend-paying ETF.

MARGIN

When it comes to margin, our advice is simple. DON'T do it. The risk is too great.

While margin has the potential to increase your gains massively, essentially you are borrowing money from your broker to fund your stock purchase. If the trade goes well, and the market doesn't correct, dragging prices down, you won't have problems. But what if the position goes against you? A "margin call" can lead to forced sales and your account could be wiped out.

A good thing about options trading is that you can't borrow money to buy options. However, options have leverage ingrained within them. You control 100 shares of the underlying by buying a single contract. The problem, from a margin risk standpoint, is that you can buy more stock on margin to increase the number of CCs you can initiate.

For example, you can go on margin and buy 200 shares of AT&T instead of 100 with your cash. This will allow you to write two CCs instead of just one. If the price of AT&T rises, you'll make a windfall. However, if it falls, you're going to be out a lot of money.

Leverage with The Wheel can destabilize the rest of your portfolio, and it's not worth the risk. Remember that The Wheel should comprise approximately 10% of your overall portfolio. It doesn't make sense losing your portfolio because you mismanaged 10% of it. That's like losing your house because you couldn't take care of the garage.

Is there any situation when the use of leverage makes sense? Not really. You're already using leverage when you buy options, so it doesn't make sense to push it even higher. The other issue is margin fees. Every broker charges you interest for borrowing money, and takes the money out of your account. If your position lasts for long enough, those fees will prove to be too high a bar to cross.

Remember that your CC is going to last for a while and everyday that you hang on to a margined position will cost you interest. This means your effective profit price is increasing all the time and your CC is actively hindering you from making money. The premium you earn from writing an OTM CC isn't going to help you overcome this hurdle, even if you roll the position upwards and keep prolonging it. In short, it's a bad bet and you should stay away from it.

The next problem with margin is that you need to maintain a decent amount of equity in your account to keep holding on to the position. Maintenance margin requirements mean even more of your cash needs to be tied up in the position, and you'll also expose the rest of your portfolio to margin risk.

This is why we advise against going on margin to initiate The Wheel. The gains aren't worth the risk you'll undertake. Instead of trying to get rich quick with margin, it's best to slowly compound your wealth. Over time, you'll outstrip the get-rich-quick crowd, and your gains per trade will be worth more than their entire accounts.

STRATEGY CHOICES

If you have a small account (less than $10,000), then capital management becomes critical. Your account will experience a ton of volatility because your positions will be heavily concentrated. Good capital management will make it easier for you to ride out the crests and dips.

Note that good capital management doesn't automatically equal diversification. In fact, it's a bad idea to diversify your holdings in a small account. None of your positions will be large enough to make an impact on your portfolio and it'll remain stuck in place. The key to good capital management is to understand what you're getting into before you place your position.

This means understanding the stock you're investing in. Even more importantly, you should understand the strategy you're investing in. Many strategies are volatile and require significant amounts of capital. Although The Wheel requires relatively small amounts of capital, it isn't the cheapest to put into action. It isn't the most volatile out there, but it can produce some surprises every now and then.

This happens because of the options legs in the strategy. Assignment can cause volatility swings as the value of your portfolio will rise according to the strike price of your options. If the volatility is too much, or if you aren't comfortable setting aside a lot of capital for The Wheel, consider alternative trading strategies.

For example, credit spreads are great option strategies if you want to put a little capital into options for producing gains and income. We've written extensively about implementing them in our book *Credit Spreads for Beginners*

The other thing to note about volatility is that, as your account grows in size, you need to diversify away from a handful of instruments. Take care to not diversify too much. However, you should invest in other asset classes as your portfolio grows. The last thing you want is huge swings in your portfolio because you're far too concentrated.

Entering positions is also tricky with large portfolios. Your average ticket size will be high and with many stocks, this can have an impact on the price spread. For example, an order of 10 shares of AT&T is unlikely to move the needle. However, an order of 10,000 shares (100 options contracts) will definitely move prices a bit. While this isn't anywhere near institutional ticket sizes, you increase the risk of receiving poor entry prices.

The problem is compounded when you want to exit your trade. In this situation, your profits are directly tied to your exit price. As you exit large positions, the market will move and the amount of money you can collect will change rapidly. The best way to mitigate your risk in these situations is to use limit and stop orders.

A limit order guarantees you'll be filled at a certain price (not quantity) while a stop guarantees you'll be filled for a certain quantity (not price). On entry, using a limit order makes a lot of sense since this will help you manage your entry prices. Fix a limit price and enter your order. If your broker doesn't fill it entirely, then enter a new limit order with a different price.

On exit, you can use either a limit or a stop order. A stop order is great if you want to exit the position immediately. The prices you receive will be at market, which increases profit risk. However, if you're exiting before an impending volatile event, exiting using a stop is the best move. You can also exit using a limit, as well, if exiting immediately isn't a priority. Note that it might take you longer than usual to exit your position because of the size of your positions.

While all options strategies, including The Wheel, are scalable, there is a limit to how well they'll work with large amounts of money. If you manage to reach an account capital value that's in the millions, you'll find that gathering enough positions to generate the same amount of return will be tough. This is because you'll have to buy many more options and stock to execute The Wheel and this will put the market on notice.

You won't be able to enter and exit at will, and therefore you won't be able to replicate your performance when you had lower capital levels. Here's where your choice of strategy comes into play. The best strategy for large amounts of capital is a long-term buy and hold. Strategies that rely on entering and exiting the market quickly don't scale well.

The lesson for you to take here is: Move more of your capital into long-term buy and hold strategies and ditch your reliance on short-term ones. The Wheel is great in this regard because you can switch it to focus on a long-term strategy. You can write your CSPs close to the money, get assigned, and start writing CCs on your long-term holdings.

Another tip that we'll share with you is to split your accounts, using perhaps $50,000 as a maximum account balance. As your account size grows, you'll have to worry about brokerage risk as well. What if the broker you're trading with happens to go under? In this era, when Wall Street banks can fail, there's no guarantee that your broker is immune to a crisis. The best thing is to have multiple brokerage accounts and allocate no more than $50,000 to each account. You can even hold different stocks in different accounts.

Sound money management requires discipline, as we noted in the beginning of this chapter. Make sure you follow all of these tips and you'll be just fine. Do not give in to the temptation of increasing your risk per trade to more than 10% of your account. Doing so will put the rest of your portfolio at risk. Keep collecting premiums and earning a steady return. You'll eventually grow your account to a formidable size and your returns will increase accordingly.

CAN YOU EXECUTE THE WHEEL IN AN IRA

A common question our readers have for us is whether The Wheel can be executed within an IRA. The answer is yes, you can execute it within an IRA.

Because The Wheel is classified as a defined risk trade, it's possible to implement it in your IRA. Many investors are mistaken when they believe that all options trades are banned in an IRA. The truth is that unlimited risk options trades are banned. You cannot sell options without covering them. Selling an option implies you're opening yourself up to unlimited risk. If it isn't covered, your broker won't allow you to open that position.

The CC and CSP are defined risk trades. With the former, your long stock position covers risk while your cash covers it in the latter case. These strategies are perfectly acceptable in an IRA. Just be sure that you understand the tax implications of using The Wheel Strategy with your IRA funds.

Reverse Wheels

The next common question we receive is whether a reverse Wheel is worth implementing. A reverse Wheel is when you sell a call on a falling stock and aim to profit from the downward move in its price. Theoretically, this is possible. However, you'll find it tough to execute in practice. This is because the markets go up in the long term.

There's also additional volatility you'll have to deal with when you go bearish. Bearish moves are sharper and shorter than bullish ones. This means the IV in your stocks will be naturally high and you'll have more of a rollercoaster ride to deal with. It's far better to stick to going long and implementing The Wheel as it was intended. Use bearish periods to add to your long stock holding and keep collecting more premiums.

In bearish markets you can get away with writing CCs closer to the underlying price. You'll collect greater premiums doing this and boost your returns.

11

INCREASE YOUR ODDS OF SUCCESS

The Wheel seems like a straightforward strategy to execute, and, in fact, it is. However, that doesn't mean you should underestimate its complexity. Even the simplest of strategies has nuances that can trip you up. For this reason, we're going to give you a few tips and pointers so that you can get better at executing The Wheel.

One of the biggest mistakes you can make in the market is to jump in without taking the time to prepare beforehand. Preparation extends well beyond researching the stock you're going to trade. You need to prepare yourself mentally as well. Many newer investors underestimate the effects that live markets have on them and end up stumbling.

Let's begin by looking at how you should prepare yourself before you begin executing The Wheel with real money.

PAPER TRADE

Before you begin trading with live money, it's important that you trade with paper money or simulate your trades on a platform first. Paper trading allows you to play around with the strategy with almost no negative consequences. We say "almost" because many traders paper trade with incorrect motives.

You should use paper trading as a way of getting to know how you'll react in real time. You should treat it as seriously as a real-time trade. This prepares your mind for the rigors of live trading and you can transfer your skills seamlessly when you begin working with real money. If you aren't serious about it, you'll end up losing money when you go live.

Even if you're an experienced options trader, we encourage you to paper trade before going live. This is how every successful trader operates and it makes sense that you should follow this path as well. There are many platforms that allow you to simulate your trades.

Check if your broker provides a free platform to do this. The most popular ones are E*Trade's options simulation platform. You'll need an E*Trade account to use this. If you've already invested in long-term positions in the stock market, you can use this for free. Other brokers include TD Ameritrade's thinkorswim platform. If you don't want to sign up with any broker, you can use Investopedia's stock simulator platform which will give you $100,000 in virtual money. Note that it's best to sign up with a broker's platform in order to get to get comfortable with the look and feel of their options screens.

This book serves as an excellent platform for you to begin trading The Wheel. However, real understanding comes from executing the strategy, not just reading about it. You need to practice your skills regularly and execute your paper trades as perfectly as possible. Set aside some time every day to practice your skills. This time should be separate from the times when you're executing your paper trades.

Review the concepts presented in this book and seek to expand your knowledge. For example, you should become comfortable with correlating the VIX and options deltas to trade opportunities. You need to familiarize yourself with the technical analysis methods we've shown in this book. Practice and review these for around 15-20 minutes every day.

Remember that the most important part of the entire process is selecting the right stock to run the wheel on in the first place. So if you're strapped for time and only have the chance to really go deep on one of the concepts we've discussed, make sure it's selecting stocks.

PREPARE YOURSELF MENTALLY

Many investors assume they'll automatically execute their strategies perfectly in the market when the time comes. Once they have positions in the market, they realize that handling the mental swings is tough. A good investor devises their own plans to mitigate these emotional swings.

It's important for you to remain invested until you've seen your strategy to its fruition. Trades take time to work and withdrawing your position before it has had a chance to work is a great way to stagnate.

Prepare yourself mentally by visualizing all of the negative and positive scenarios that could occur before you place a trade. See yourself remaining calm and executing your strategy perfectly. Make sure you have thought through your potential moves – will you roll? Close?

It also helps if you lead a disciplined lifestyle. Don't roll out of bed to place trades in the market and don't expect to place good trades if you're going through tough times in your personal life.

Putting money into the market can place a great deal of stress on your mind and you need to be in top shape to tackle the markets. It's fine to take a break and walk away from the trading screen if nothing is making sense to you or if you feel as if you "have" to place a trade. FOMO is a leading creator of losses in the market.

Always monitor yourself psychologically before putting your money in the market. Exercise regularly, follow good nutritional habits, and get plenty of sleep. Basic self-care will help you remain in the best possible state and will increase your odds of success. Good habits will put you in the best position to grow your wealth.

CHOOSE THE RIGHT INSTRUMENTS

Your choice of investment instrument is critical to your success. Most beginner investors try to implement The Wheel with as many random stocks and ETFs as possible. This is a scattershot approach and is unlikely to bring you any real results. The key to investment success is to create situations where you need to exert the least amount of mental effort towards mundane tasks.

Your mental energy should be focused on execution as much as possible, instead of having to worry about the characteristics of the instrument you're operating in. For example, we highlighted the case of USO being a poor choice for The Wheel. A quick read of the ETF's objectives would alert you that the managers speculate in oil futures, and it's not a good candidate. The thing to do is to identify a handful of instruments during your paper trading sessions, and stick to them like glue.

This way, you'll learn their subtleties and how they behave in different situations. If the VIX shoots up, does the instrument behave erratically? Or does it remain stable? Does the stock generally move within a range, or does it tend to decline more often than it rises? Does it have a pattern such as 3 days up followed by three down?

Note that a decline can be a gentle one while a price increase could be a forceful yet sporadic one. Such stocks are a nightmare to make money with since they don't do much and whenever they do something, they do it erratically. Getting to know your instruments beforehand is a key part of successful paper trading.

Begin by identifying three or four instruments that are good candidates. Then paper trade these instruments for at least six months to get to know them well. Note that if you're running monthly options, that's six to eight trades per instrument, which isn't a lot. If you've made money at the end of this period, then you should move that instrument to live trading.

You'll find that it'll be tough to make money with certain stocks. This isn't the strategy's fault or even a problem with your execution. It's a case of the instrument simply being unsuited to The Wheel. Many traders give up on perfectly viable strategies because they fail to take the instrument's suitability into account.

How many instruments should you have in your Wheel House? This depends on the amount of time you are willing to invest. Three or 4 should be maximum if you plan to spend only 15-30 minutes a day evaluating the market and your portfolio. Running The Wheel with too many instruments can cause you to reserve a lot of cash. It might be better for you to invest that cash for the long term, instead of trying to earn some option premiums with it.

Generally speaking, running The Wheel with just two or three instruments works well. Start by paper trading these instruments and move them to live trading only when you've made steady money with them. Don't randomly bring instruments into the live money account without testing them for suitability first.

Plan For Earnings Announcements

As we discussed earlier, you should pay close attention to the earnings announcement dates of your investments. If the stock tends to bounce up or down on earnings, you may want to close your options positions before the announcement. For this reason, you should choose companies that don't all have announce around the same time. This means you can always have a Wheel in operation and you'll make money consistently. If the earnings dates of all the stocks you're operating in are clustered, you'll have to suspend trading for four months every year. That's one quarter eliminated.

Of course, if you decided to trade ETF's, earnings announcements are not a factor. However, don't resort to ETFs thinking you've eliminated an area of concern. ETFs can be good choices because many do not have sharp price fluctuations. However, they tend to be higher priced than individual stocks and therefore require more capital.

WEEKLY OPTIONS

You can also move to weekly options as we've mentioned. If your aim is to earn more money, then a weekly expiration strategy will work very well. However, you'll have to be more active managing your positions. Weekly options also prevent you from capturing the full extent of theta decay and your per position earnings will be low.

To overcome this hurdle, you'll need to operate in more stocks, which means more money laid out for The Wheel. At the very least, you'll need four stocks to operate in. There are volatility concerns you need to factor in as well. Make sure you enter new positions on a Monday and exit on a Friday.

The weekend witnesses major volatility events, so choosing to have an open position over this time is inadvisable. This means choosing the right instruments is even more critical. The margin of error with weeklies is a lot less, so it's advisable to scale into it. Start by writing one weekly option and then running it for a few months before trying it with another instrument.

Gently scale into weeklies like this and you'll increase your chances of success.

CONCLUSION

"I fear not the man who has practiced 10,000 kicks once, but I fear the man who has practiced one kick 10,000 times."

— BRUCE LEE

Mastery over anything takes time and effort. The Wheel is a simple strategy, but don't underestimate it because of this. You'll need to spend time practicing it well before you can expect to make money. The other thing to note is that The Wheel is designed to earn you steady income that you can compound over a long period of time.

It isn't a strategy that will make you a ton of money overnight. Those kinds of strategies are extremely volatile and most people cannot make them work due to the mental stress they place. The Wheel is a straightforward and easy-to-understand strategy that you can use on any stock or ETF to earn more money long term.

The key to making it work is to operate in instruments that you'd be happy to own. Don't adopt a scattershot approach with a view to capturing the highest premium or making the most money. The Wheel works best when you use it with a handful of stocks. It's far better to do deep and narrow than wide and shallow. Follow the tips we've outlined in this book to identify the best stocks and scale into them intelligently.

Take care to pay attention to the VIX before you initiate a position. Many investors focus only on the IV and neglect the overall market's position. IV can change in a hurry if it's opposed to the VIX. Remaining in touch with the larger market and keeping up with volatility events is the key to initiating good positions. Often, individual stocks adopt volatility characteristics of the larger market due to traders migrating to them in the short term.

The great thing about The Wheel is that you don't need knowledge of options Greeks beyond delta and theta. Even with these Greeks, you only need to understand the basics of how they work. You can find them on any option chain easily and can interpret them using the lessons you've learned in this book.

Choosing the right instruments is critical for your success. There are both fundamental and technical factors to take into account before you initiate a position. We've covered these requirements in detail in this book. Make sure you thoroughly understand them before proceeding.

Stay away from media darlings or hot stocks. As a rule of thumb, any stock or instrument that's being talked about in the media or by Wall Street analysts is a bad bet for you. It's much better to stick to boring stocks that aren't being hailed in the news or by the Stocktwits crowd. Boring is good when it comes to investing. It means you've invested in instruments that are reliable and producing regular income for you.

When executing the strategy, make sure you follow the steps we've outlined in the relevant chapter in this book. Remember that the steps you follow will depend on your investment objectives. Short-term investors should seek to avoid assignment and focus on earning premiums. This means their CSP needs to be at a reasonable distance away from the money. Long-term investors can use The Wheel as a great way to get paid to enter their positions and keep earning premiums on them through the CC leg of the trade.

Short-term investors should be careful when rolling their options. Pay attention to the credit and debit terms of the trade before choosing to roll your position. Rolling is a great way to extend your trade, but it shouldn't be your default option.

Above all else, remain patient with The Wheel and take the time to fully study it before diving into it. Practice your skills properly before trading with live money. You'll notice the difference in your results when you follow the tips we've provided you in this book. Patience is an asset for every investor, not matter how long your investing timeframe.

So how much can you earn when you add The Wheel to your regular portfolio?

If you begin with $5,000 and earn a return of 20% over 10 years (which you can, thanks to the premiums you'll earn with The Wheel), you'll be left with a principal of $30,958. Start with $10,000 and you'll end up with $61,917. Start with $20,000 and you'll have $123,834.

We wish you the best of luck with your investments!

If you have any questions, or would like further clarification, you can email us at admin@freemanpublications.com. We answer every single reader's email.

One final word from us. If this book has helped you in any way, we'd appreciate it if you left a review on Amazon.

Reviews are the lifeblood of our business. We read every single one and incorporate your feedback into our future book projects.

To leave an Amazon review, go to

https://freemanpublications.com/leaveareview

"The most successful people in life are the ones who ask questions. They're always learning. They're always growing. They're always pushing."

Robert Kiyosaki

CONTINUING YOUR JOURNEY

Like Robert Kiyosaki said on the previous page, "The most successful people in life are always learning, growing, and asking questions."

Which is why we created our investing community, aptly named **How To NOT Lose Money in the Stock Market**, so that like-minded individuals could get together to share ideas and learn from each other.

We regularly run giveaways, share wins from our readers, and you'll be the first to know when our new books are released.

It's 100% free, and there are no requirements to join, except for the willingness to learn.

You can join us on Facebook by going to
http://freemanpublications.com/facebook

OTHER BOOKS BY FREEMAN PUBLICATIONS (AVAILABLE ON AMAZON & AUDIBLE)

The 8-Step Beginner's Guide to Value Investing: Featuring 20 for 20 - The 20 Best Stocks & ETFs to Buy and Hold for The Next 20 Years

Bear Market Investing Strategies: 37 Recession-Proof Ideas to Grow Your Wealth - Including Inverse ETFs, Put Options, Gold & Cryptocurrency

Iron Condor Options for Beginners: A Smart, Safe Method to Generate an Extra 25% Per Year with Just 2 Trades Per Month

Covered Calls for Beginners: A Risk-Free Way to Collect "Rental Income" Every Single Month on Stocks You Already Own

Credit Spread Options for Beginners: Turn Your Most Boring Stocks into Reliable Monthly Paychecks using Call, Put & Iron Butterfly Spreads - Even If The Market is Doing Nothing

 Dividend Growth Investing: Get a Steady 8% Per Year Even in a Zero Interest Rate World - Featuring The 13 Best High Yield Stocks, REITs, MLPs and CEFs For Retirement Income

The Only Bitcoin Investing Book You'll Ever Need: An Absolute Beginner's Guide to the Cryptocurrency Which Is Changing the World and Your Finances in 2021 & Beyond

REFERENCES

AAPL Short Put 45 DTE Cash-Secured Options Backtest. (2019, October 4). Spintwig. https://spintwig.com/aapl-short-put-45-dte-options-backtest/

Artemis Capital Management LP. (2016). *Star Wars Convexity.* https://thewaiterspad.files.wordpress.com/2017/06/4291d-artemis_starwarsvolatility.pdf

SPY Short Put 45 DTE Cash-Secured Options Backtest. (2019, June 10). Spintwig. https://spintwig.com/spy-short-put-strategy-performance/

Tully, S. (2020, December 2). *Tesla's biggest profit center is dangerously close to running out of power.* Fortune. https://fortune.com/2020/09/30/tesla-profit-revenue-environmental-credits-elon-musk

REFERENCES

All Images by Freeman Publications

Made in the USA
Columbia, SC
31 May 2023

17578806R00093